To Kill Cow Means To End Human Civilization

By
Dr. Sahadeva dasa

B.COM., ACA., ICWA., PHD
Chartered Accountant

Soul Science University Press
www.cowism.com

"The time will come when men will look on the murder of animals as they now look on the murder of men."
-Leonardo da Vinci

Readers interested in the subject matter of this
book are invited to correspond with the publisher at:
SoulScienceUniversity@gmail.com +91 98490 95990

To order a copy write to chandra@rgbooks.co.in
or buy online: at www.rgbooks.co.in

First Edition: August 2009

Soul Science University Press expresses its gratitude to the Bhaktivedanta Book
Trust International (BBT), for the use of quotes by His Divine Grace
A.C.Bhaktivedanta Swami Prabhupada.
Copyright Bhaktivedanta Book Trust International (BBT)

ISBN 978-81-909760-2-2

Price in India: Rs.100/-

Published by:
Dr. Sahadeva dasa for Soul Science University Press

Designed by:
Sri Sailesh Ijmulwar
waar creatives, Hyderabad, waar.ad@gmail.com

Printed by:
Rainbow Print Pack, Hyderabad

Dedicated to....

His Divine Grace A.C.Bhaktivedanta Swami Prabhupada

"Krishna has given her the grass to eat. She's not interfering with your food. What right you have got to kill? You have got your own food. The cow has got the grass for her food. That is nature's way, by God's will, that a cow gives forty pounds, fifty pounds milk daily, but she does not drink. Although it is her milk, no, it gives you, human society: "You take. But don't kill me. Let me live. I am eating only grass." Just see. And the civilized men killing them, killing them. Without touching your foodstuff, the cow is eating the grass which is given by God, immense grass, and they are giving you the finest foodstuff, milk. Just after your birth you have only milk to drink, either mother's milk... Nowadays, mothers do not supply milk. That is also to be supplied by the cow. So from the very beginning of my life I am subsisting by the foodstuff given by mother, cow, and when I am grown up, I kill. This is my gratitude. Just see. And they are called civilized. Less than lowest animal, naradhama. They are called naradhama, lowest of the mankind. Those who are killing cows, maintaining slaughterhouses, they are lowest of the mankind. They are not human being. Less than animals. They have no gratitude. And they want peace. Just see the fun."

(Lecture on Srimad-Bhagavatam, Los Angeles, September 19, 1972)

By The Same Author

Oil - Final Countdown To A Global Crisis And Its Solutions

End of Modern Civilization and Alternative Future

Cow And Humanity - Made For Each Other

*Capitalism Communism And Cowism - A New Economics
For The 21st Century*

Cows Are Cool - Love 'Em !

Wondrous Glories of Vraja

Modern Foods - Stealing Years From Your Life

*Noble Cow - Munching Grass, Looking Curious And Just Hanging
Around*

Lets Be Friends - A Curious, Calm Cow

We Feel - Just Like You Do

(More information on availability at the back)

Contents

Preface   VI

Section I : Life Is Sacred

Animals Have A Soul   5

Mother And Child - A Story   7

Religious Philosophy And Attitude Towards Animals   9

Hunter And The Sage   13

Legalized Terrorism - Animal Abuse And Killing   34

Section II : Why Do Indians Consider Cow As Sacred?

Sacred Cow - A Dumb Indian Idea?   40

Cow Gives And Gives And Gives   57

Humanity Owes Milk Debt To Cows   69

Cow - The Provider of All Human Necessities   85

Cow - A Symbol of Innocence, Purity And Magnanimity   104

To Further The Cause of Cow Protection   111

Preface

We are the masters of the universe and the whole creation is made to fulfill our whims - this misconception is costing us dearly. We are thinking that we can do whatever we like, everything has evolved from chaos and there is no body to check on anything we do. This is a dangerous philosophy. This is a significant shift from the traditional concepts of reverence for the cosmic world and its Creator.

Today we are treating other life forms just like inert objects. We are showing unprecedented cruelty and callousness. Cruelty has been industrialized, barbarism has been institutionalized. Today the mistreatment of animals is phenomenal, unprecedented in human history. The unspeakable treatment meted out to poor animals before they become our dinner will never go unpunished by the stringent laws of nature.

This book specifically deals with 'cow', the very representative of the aphonic creation of God. Cow is a symbol of selfless service in life and death. Our attitude towards this important animal will decide our fate. Strange it may sound or even eccentric, cow will prove to be the making or breaking point for humanity.

Already we stand at the crossroads today. Dangerous challenges are staring us in the face from environmental, ecological, moral, social, economic and health fronts. Global uncertainties are mounting and humanity's future prospects look increasingly bleak.

There is a correlation between cruelty towards animals and wars in human society. Animal slaughter and violence in human society are interrelated. 20th century saw the establishment of global networks in animal products and inhumane factory farming system. At the same time, 20th century also saw the two most brutal World Wars, the worst acts of barbarism like holocaust, gulag concentration camps, genocides and atomic bombing of Hiroshima and Nagasaki. It was the bloodiest century in human history.

Mahatma Gandhi often said, "Cow-slaughter and man-slaughter are in my opinion the two sides of the same coin."

The same sentiments were echoed by George Bernard Shaw, *"The Peace we say we are anxious for? Thus cruelty begets its offspring—War."*

Cruelty is killing us in many ways. Dr. Neal Barnard says, "The beef industry has contributed to more American deaths than all the wars of this century, all natural disasters, and all automobile accidents combined. If beef is your idea of "real food for real people", you"d better live real close to a real good hospital."

Sahadeva dasa

Dr. Sahadeva dasa
5th August 2009
Secunderabad, India

Section-I

Human or Nonhuman

Life Is Sacred

"I define terrorism as any intentional act to injure or kill a living, sentient, innocent being for scientific, political or economic purposes."

~Steve Best

"A dead cow or sheep lying in a pasture is recognized as carrion. The same sort of a carcass dressed and hung up in a butcher's stall passes as food," writes Dr. John Harvey Kellogg. Time and again, over the centuries and across the cultures, the subject of animal slaughter and flesh diet has been discussed. Also since time immemorial, many cultures have avoided animal slaughter and flesh diet. These cultures were built on the philosophy of peaceful coexistence with nature and the principle of nonviolence.

This book deals with the subject of cow but before lunging into the subject, we will examine views on life in general, from the Vedic or Indian perspective.

Life Is Sacred And All Life Forms Are Worthy of Respect

Traditional Indian or Vedic way of life teaches respect for all life forms. In their view, all living beings are born of mother nature and have an equal right to life. Indeed, in Vedic conception, animals are treated like innocent children and are meant to be given all protection. Srimad Bhagavatam, the foremost of the Vedic texts states, "One should treat animals such as deer, camels, asses, monkeys, mice, snakes, birds and flies exactly like one's own son. How little difference there actually is between children and these innocent animals." *(SB 7.14.9)*

The doctrine of reincarnation holds that every creature is a spirit

Ethics, too, are nothing but reverence for life. This is what gives me the fundamental principle of morality, namely, that good consists in maintaining, promoting, and enhancing life, and that destroying, injuring, and limiting life are evil."
-Albert Schweitzer (Civilization and Ethics, 1949)

soul that lives in one material body after another. And all life is sacred, not just the life of cow. Vedic concept is that all life forms emanate from the Supreme Life and are therefore venerable.

Each of us is an eternal spirit soul; we are not the material body that covers us. Every life form—whether bird, insect, fish, mammal, plant, or fetus—houses an individual, eternal soul as well as the Supreme Soul, who accompanies the individual soul as he transmigrates from body to body in his adventures throughout the material universe. Thus every form of life is sacred and should never be whimsically destroyed.

In fact, not only Vedic culture, but all traditional cultures teach respect for life and nature in general. It is the techno-industrial life style which is utterly callous towards life and nature.

Modern Life Is Founded on Disregard For Life and Nature

Modern life is characterized by a total lack of reverence towards life, both human and nonhuman.

In spite of the availability of so much food, billions of animals are mercilessly raised, transported and slaughtered every year. The reactions are equally severe. Human beings also die in riots, bombings and wars in the same brutal fashion.

When a few birds or cows fall sick, we murder millions of them in the name of culling. These things have no precedent in human history. This is holocaust and cold blooded murder. In God's kingdom, all beings have the right to live and one has to pay dearly for killing even an ant unnecessarily. Time is coming when people will 'cull' a whole race or country when they get infected with a disease.

Institutionalization Of Barbarism, Industrialization Of Cruelty

Cruelty has existed in human society since time immemorial but in modern times, it has become industrialized. Cruelty has taken the shape of a global industry and the world has never witnessed such institutionalization of barbarism. People always killed animals for food, entertainment or fur etc. but killing in mechanized industrial slaughterhouses is a modern invention. Animals were never transported thousands of miles for killing and neither ever existed global marketing networks in animal products.

Perhaps this millennium has been the bloodiest of all human history. For about forty years after the discovery of the New World (America), it was legal to hunt down the natives like animals. It was only in 1530 that the Pope conceded that American Indians were human!

This is what Aime Cesaire wrote in 1955 in "'Discours sur le colonialisme" while trying to put the horrors of Hitler in perspective:

"What the very Christian bourgeois of the twentieth century cannot forgive Hitler for is not the crime in itself, the crime against humanity, not the humiliation of humanity itself, but the crime against the white man...; it is the crime of having applied to Europe the colonialist actions as were borne uptil now by the Arabs, the coolies of India and the negroes of Africa."

Animals Have A Soul And They Feel Just Like We Do

Some of the world's religions erroneously propound that only human life is sacred because only humans have a soul. This is a dangerous and irrational fallacy, a completely absurd proposition. We eat, sleep, mate and defend and animals do the same. Where is the difference? We feel pain and pleasure and so they do. Our bodies are made up of flesh and blood and so are theirs. Rather animals are more 'human' in many ways. Those who claim animals have no soul are in fact the ones without a soul.

Take for example rats. They are highly sociable beings - they communicate with each other at high-frequency sounds, play together, wrestle, and love sleeping curled up together. Much like us, if they do not have companionship, they become lonely, anxious, depressed, and stressed. They become attached to each other, love their own

This killing of animals is for the non-civilized society. They cannot... They do not know how to grow food. They were killing animals. When man is advanced in his knowledge and education, why they should kill? Especially in America, we see so many nice foodstuffs. Fruits, grains, milk. And from milk, you can get hundreds of nice preparations, all nutritious.
-Srila Prabhupada (Room Conversation, July 5, 1975, Chicago)

5

families, and easily bond with their human guardians, returning as much affection as is given to them. Many rats will even "groom" their human companion's hand and would appreciate a massage, a scratch behind the ears, or even a tickle in return. Recent studies by a neuroscientist at Bowling Green State University, suggest that when rats play or are playfully tickled, they make chirping sounds that are strikingly similar to human laughter. The rats he studied also bonded socially with the human tickler and even sought to be tickled more. Young rats have a marvelous sense of fun.

Male rats will snuggle up for a cuddle and find contentment curled up in a person's lap. Rats love seeing kind people and will often bounce around waiting to be noticed and picked up. Rats can bond with their human companions to the point that if they are suddenly given away to someone else or forgotten, they can pine to death.

It is estimated that each year, tens of millions of rats and mice are killed in experiments in laboratories. With the popularity of genetic engineering, the numbers are increasing.

Anyone who has ever kept a pet can testify that animals very much have a soul, that too a warm and affectionate one.

Look at the following true stories to check it out for yourself.

"Truly man is the king of beasts, for his brutality exceeds theirs. We live by the death of others. We are burial places! I have since an early age abjured the use of meat"
- Leonardo da Vinci (1452-1519)

Mother and Child

By Venerable Wuling (A Buddhist monk), May 2008

One morning, in the spring of 2004, I opened my window blinds, sat down at my desk in front of the window, and glanced out to look at the lawn and pond. Several yards in front of the window, I saw a tiny bunny hovering over the body of a full-grown rabbit. The rabbit had apparently died in a small indentation, about a yard across, in the ground. Throughout the day, I watched as the young bunny ran back and forth over and over across the lawn chasing away a large bird that was trying to get at the dead rabbit.

When not chasing the bird, the bunny bit off mouthfuls of the tall grass growing in the indentation, went to the rabbit, and placed the grass on top of the body. The process took considerable time, as the bunny had to keep chasing off the hungry bird at the same time. The bunny was still trying to fend off the bird when I shut my window blinds that evening.

One morning in the spring of 2005, I saw a grown rabbit hop straight to the spot where the other rabbit had been buried. The rabbit rearranged what remained of the still discernible mound of grass and then hopped back the way it had come from around the side of the building. I did not see the rabbit in 2006, nor in 2007 as I was then working in another room.

It is now spring, 2008. Late Monday night, I returned to the US from two months in Australia. Tuesday, I woke up in the afternoon trying to readjust to a very different time zone. Wednesday was my first morning in about eighteen months to work at my desk in my old spot in front of the window.

The thick grass outside my window was deep and due for the weekly cutting. I could still see the spot where the rabbit had died for the grass has yet to cover the "burial mound." As I watched, I saw a rabbit come around from the side of the building and hop straight to the spot. It remained a few seconds and hopped off a bit to the left of the spot. Then it hopped straight back to the spot, rearranged some of the dead grass, paused a few seconds, and hopped right back the way it had come from around the side of the building.

Affinities span many lifetimes. They do not involve just human beings. And just as humans can be filial children, other beings can as well.

Good Bye!
By Bob White

All animals connect. It is us who disconnect. Even fish connect. I had a group of fish for 5 years. Every morning, the largest one would make a huge loop around the tank to say, "Good Morning". (It was a vertical loop, not a circling feeding loop.) As this fish was dying, I sat vigil with it for 3 days. It was barely breathing. I looked and it made the effort to make one huge vertical loop around the tank and then died. I'm sure it was saying, "Good Bye".

I thought it was important to share this story for all who think they are "saving a fish from drowning" when they eat it. I don't eat fish. They were my friends for 5 wonderful years.

Companionship
By Sue K, Philippines, March 2009

My husband and I had two guinea pigs. When one of them unexpectedly died last year, the other pig became what I can only describe as depressed. He barely ate, he barely moved. His eyes were dull, he didn't squeak anymore or show any curiosity towards anything. We wanted to mourn the loss of our little pig friend for a while, but we ended up adopting another guinea pig from the humane society within days because we were so worried for our other pig. Within hours of the new pig being in the house (not even in the same enclosure yet, due to quarantine precautions), the bereft pig perked right up and began eating and squeaking again. It was amazing to witness. Both pigs are still very happy together, over a year later.

Some rascals put forward the theory that an animal has no soul or is something like dead stone. In this way they rationalize that there is no sin in animal killing. Actually animals are not dead stone, but the killers of animals are stone-hearted. Consequently no reason or philosophy appeals to them. They continue keeping slaughterhouses and killing animals.
-Srila Prabhupada (Srimad-Bhagavatam 4.26.9)

Animals are our brothers and sisters on this planet and I am honored to have these little pigs as companions in our home. *They teach me much about being content with food, shelter, warmth and companionship.*

Religious Philosophy And Attitude Towards Animals

Whether we are actively religious or not, religious belief permeates the very fabric of our existence. Namely, it influences, if not directly shapes, our personal, economic, social and ethical life. It is then only logical to surmise that religion also influences how we, individually and collectively, treat animals.

What role does religion play in shaping our attitude towards the animal world? One answer was proposed in 1967 by UCLA History Professor Lynn White, Jr., who wrote an article entitled, "The Historical Roots of Our Ecological Crisis" (Science 155, 1967). In this article, he said that the Western world's attitudes towards animals and nature were shaped by the Judeo-Christian tradition (he also included Islam and Marxism within this overall tradition). This tradition, White wrote, involved the concept of a world created solely for the benefit of man: "God planned all of creation explicitly for man's benefit and rule: no item in the physical creation had any purpose save to serve man's purposes." Along with this, Western

Christianity separated humans from nature. In older religious traditions, humans were seen as part of nature, rather than the ruler of nature. And in animistic religions, there was believed to be a spirit in every tree, mountain or spring, and all had to be respected. In contrast with paganism and Eastern religions, Christianity "not only established a dualism of man and nature but also insisted that it is God's will that man exploit nature for his proper ends." White noted that Christianity was a complex faith, and different branches of it differ in their outlook. But in general, he proposed that Christianity, and Western civilization as a whole, held a view of nature that separated humans from the rest of the natural world, and encouraged exploitation of it for our own ends.

The emergence of Christianity, many, like White believe, marked the moment humans broke away from previously common held beliefs that all beings, all forms of life, including plants, had spirits (or souls).

"In Antiquity every tree, every spring, every stream, every hill had its own genius loci, its guardian spirit," he wrote. And Christianity changed all that, he believed. Man was created in God's image, Christians believed, and notably Man was created at the end of Creation and humans therefore inherited the Earth. "By destroying pagan animism," White wrote, "Christianity made it possible to exploit nature in a mood of indifference to the feelings of natural objects."

There has been much discussion on Lynn White's articles but in general these questionable ideologies are responsible, at least in part, for the phenomenal cruelty towards animals we see in the modern world.

Also this misleading religious view has influenced other disciplines like science, ethics, economics, education and public policy.

> *"All things bright and beautiful*
> *All creatures great and small*
> *All things wise and wonderful*
> *The Lord God made them all"*
> *-Frances Alexander'*

Bishnoism

How religion influences our dealing with animals and natural world can be seen from the example of Bishnoism. It is a subsect of vedic religion which originated in the desert of Rajasthan, India, in the 15th century. Bishnoism emphasizes living in complete harmony with our natural world. It teaches love, peace, kindness, simple life, honesty, compassion and forgiveness.

Living in the inhospitable desert terrain, Bishnois have been fiercely protecting the forests and wild life in their area to follow the teachings of their Guru Jambheshwarji. For Bishnois, caring for God's creation is their prime dharma or duty. Time to time, their faith was tested by rulers, poachers and others, but Bishnois always protected the nature, even at the cost of their lives.

In 1730, 363 Bishnois were killed when they opposed cutting of Khejari trees. They hugged the trees and said, "sir santhe runkh rahe to bhi sasto jan", which means that if a tree can be saved by sacrificing one's head, even then its a good deal. These trees were being cut at the order of the king, Raja Abhay Singh. The firewood was required to burn lime stone for the construction of his palace.

Even today these people will starve to feed other hungry creatures. Women will breast feed a wild animal calf if its mother dies. In Bishnoi communities, exotic wild animals roam freely. They fight with armed poachers to protect these animals.

Bishnoism presents a sharp contrast to Western way of living with their utter disregard for nature and life in general.

> "I do feel that spiritual progress does demand at some stage that we should cease to kill our fellow creatures for the satisfaction of our bodily wants."
> - Gandhi

Communities like Bishnois, once scorned for being backward, will be hailed for teaching us a valuable lesson in harmonious living.

Jainism

The Jain tradition has existed in tandem with Vedic tradition in India since 800 BC. Jains developed their own sacred texts and follow the authority of itinerant monks and nuns who wander throughout India preaching the essential principles and practices of the faith. Jainism holds some interesting potential for ecological thinking, though its final goal transcends earthly concerns i.e., ascending to the realm above earth and heaven.

At the core of Jain faith lies five vows that dictate the daily life of Jains. These five vows, which inspired and influenced Mahatma Gandhi, are nonviolence (ahimsa), truthfulness (satya), not stealing (asteya), sexual restraint (brahmacarya), and nonpossession (aparigraha). One adheres to these vows in order to minimize harm to all possible life-forms. For observant Jains, to hurt any being results in the thickening of one's karma, obstructing advancement toward liberation. To reduce karma and prevent its further accrual, Jains avoid activities associated with violence and follow a vegetarian diet. The advanced monks and nuns will sweep their path to avoid harming insects and also work at not harming even one sensed beings such as bacteria and water.

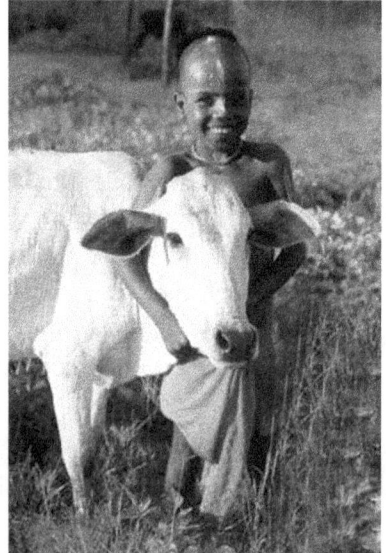

The worldview of the Jains might be characterized as a biocosmology due to their perception of the "livingness" of the world.

Bhagavata Dharma

Vedic tradition is also known as Sanatana or Bhagavata dharma.

Compassion for all living beings forms the basis of this Bhagavata dharma. Bhagavata vision of equality is explained in Gita (5.18)

vidya-vinaya-sampanne
brahmane gavi hastini
suni caiva sva-pake ca
panditah sama-darsinah

The humble sages, by virtue of true knowledge, see with equal vision a learned and gentle brahmana, a cow, an elephant, a dog and a dog-eater.

Bhagavad-gita (6.30) mentions "For one who sees Me everywhere and who sees everything in Me, I am never lost nor is he ever lost to Me." So a follower of Bhagavata dharma perceives the presence of the Supreme Lord in all living beings. Srila Prabhupada explains, "In the Vedic concept of grhastha [householder] life it is recommended that a householder see that even a lizard or a snake living in his house should not starve. Even these lower creatures should be given food, and certainly all humans should be. It is recommended that the grhastha, before taking his lunch, stand on the road and declare, "If anyone is still hungry, please come! Food is ready!" If there is no response, then the proprietor of the household takes his lunch... And these things are explained in Srimad-Bhagavatam, that this world is also God's kingdom and all living entities, they are God's sons. So everyone has got the right to take advantage of his father's property. This is Bhagavata communism. The communists are thinking in terms of their own country. But a devotee, thinks in terms of all living entities, wherever he is, either in the sky or in the land or in the water."

We can quote a nice story from Skanda Purana illustrating the Vedic conception of compassion for all living creatures.

Hunter And The Sage

Once upon a time the great saint Narada went to Prayaga to bathe at the holy confluence. On the way he saw that a deer was lying in

"As often as Herman had witnessed the slaughter of animals and fish, he always had the same thought:in their behaviour toward creatures, all men were Nazis"
-Isaac Bashevis Singer

the forest and that it was pierced by an arrow. It had broken legs and was twisting due to much pain. Farther ahead, Narada Muni saw a boar pierced by an arrow. Its legs were also broken, and it was twisting in pain. When he went farther, he saw a rabbit suffering similarly. Narada Muni was greatly pained at heart to see living entities suffer so. When Narada Muni advanced farther, he saw a hunter behind a tree. This hunter was holding arrows, and he was ready to kill more animals. The hunter's body was blackish. He had reddish eyes, and he appeared fierce. It was as if the superintendent of death, Yamaraja, was standing there with bows and arrows in his hands. When Narada Muni left the forest path and went to the hunter, all the animals immediately saw him and fled. When all the animals fled, the hunter wanted to chastise Narada with abusive language, but due to Narada's presence, he could not utter anything abusive.

The hunter addressed Narada Muni: 'O gosvami! O great saintly person! Why have you left the general path through the forest to come to me? Simply by seeing you, all the animals I was aiming at have now fled.' Narada Muni replied, 'Leaving the path, I have come to you to settle a doubt that is in my mind. I was wondering whether all the boars and other animals that are half-killed belong to you.' The hunter replied in affirmative. Narada Muni then inquired, 'Why did you not kill the animals completely? Why did you half-kill them by piercing their bodies with arrows?'

The hunter replied, 'My dear saintly person, my name is Mrgari, enemy of animals. My father taught me to kill them in that way.

When a human kills an animal for food, he is neglecting his own hunger for justice. Man prays for mercy, but is unwilling to extend it to others. Why should man then expect mercy from God? It's unfair to expect something that you are not willing to give.
-*Isaac Bashevis Singer*

14

'When I see half-killed animals suffer, I feel great pleasure.'

Narada Muni then told the hunter, 'I have one thing to beg of you.' The hunter replied, 'You may take whatever animals or anything else you would like. I have many skins if you would like them. I shall give you either a deerskin or a tiger skin.'

Narada Muni said, 'I do not want any of the skins. I am only asking one thing from you in charity. 'I beg you that from this day on you will kill animals completely and not leave them half-dead.'

The hunter replied, 'My dear sir, what are you asking of me? What is wrong with the animals' lying there half-killed? Will you please explain this to me?' Narada Muni replied, 'If you leave the animals half-dead, you are purposefully giving them pain. Therefore you will have to suffer in retaliation. My dear hunter, your business is killing animals. That is a slight offense on your part, but when you consciously give them unnecessary pain by leaving them half-dead, you incur very great sins. All the animals that you have killed and given unnecessary pain will kill you one after the other in your next life and in life after life.'

In this way, through the association of the great sage Narada Muni, the hunter was a little convinced of his sinful activity. He therefore became somewhat afraid due to his offenses. The hunter then admitted that he was convinced of his sinful activity, and he said, 'I have been taught this business from my very childhood. Now I am wondering how I can become freed from these unlimited volumes of sinful activity. My dear sir, please tell me how I can be relieved from the reactions of my sinful life. Now I fully surrender unto you and fall down at your lotus feet. Please deliver me from sinful reactions.'

Narada Muni assured the hunter, 'If you listen to my instructions, I shall find the way you can be liberated.' The hunter then said, 'My dear sir, whatever you say I shall do.' Narada immediately ordered him, 'First of all, break your bow. Then I shall tell you what is to be done.' The hunter replied, 'If I break my bow, how shall I maintain myself?' Narada Muni replied, 'Do not worry. I shall supply all your food every day.'

Being thus assured by the great sage Narada Muni, the hunter broke his bow, immediately fell down at the saint's lotus feet and fully surrendered. After this, Narada Muni raised him with his hand and gave him instructions for spiritual advancement.

Narada Muni then advised the hunter, 'Return home and distribute whatever riches you have to the pure brahmanas who know the Absolute Truth. After thus distributing all your riches, both you and your wife should leave home, taking only one cloth to wear. Leave your home and go to the river. There you should construct a small cottage, and in front of the cottage you should grow a tulasi plant on a raised platform. After planting the tulasi tree before your house, you should daily circumambulate that tulasi plant, serve her by giving her water and other things, and continuously chant the Hare Krsna maha-mantra. I shall send sufficient food to you both every day. You can take as much food as you want.'

The three animals that were half-killed were then brought to their consciousness by the sage Narada. Indeed, the animals got up and swiftly fled. When the hunter saw the half-killed animals flee, he was certainly struck with wonder. He then offered his respectful obeisances to the sage Narada and returned home.

After all this, Narada Muni went to his destination. The news that the hunter had become a Vaisnava spread all over the village. Indeed, all the villagers brought alms and presented them to the Vaisnava who was formerly a hunter. In one day enough food was brought for ten or twenty people, but the hunter and his wife would accept only as much as they could eat.

One day, while speaking to his friend Parvata Muni, Narada Muni requested him to go with him to see his disciple the hunter. When the saintly sages came to the hunter's place, the hunter could see them coming from a distance. With great alacrity the hunter began to run toward his spiritual master, but he could not fall down and offer obeisances because ants were running hither and thither around his feet. Seeing the ants, the hunter whisked them away with a piece of cloth. After thus clearing the ants from the ground, he fell down flat to offer his obeisances.

Narada Muni said, 'My dear hunter, such behavior is not at all astonishing. A man in devotional service is automatically nonviolent. He is the best of gentlemen. O hunter, good qualities like nonviolence, which you have developed, are not very astonishing, for those engaged in the Lord's devotional service are never inclined to give pain to others because of envy.'

Truth About Vedic Sacrifices

Vedic society was a strictly vegetarian society because a vegetarian diet is conducive to higher spiritual realization. Meat eating is one of the greatest obstacles on the path of spiritual progress. Despite farfetched interpretations, no scripture in the world recommends meat eating—although some scriptures may make a concession for individuals who are unable to control their tongue.

In the Vedic system, animal sacrifices are classified into two categories. First category is for testing the efficacy of mantras chanted in a fire sacrifice. Under this system, an old animal is sacrificed and by the power of mantras, it is revived back into a young, healthy animal in a process which is completely painless. This rejuvenation, if carried out successfully, determines the accuracy of the chants and successful completion of the fire sacrifice. Vedas prohibit such animal

sacrifices in modern times as it is not possible to revive dead animals anymore due to a lack of qualified priests.

The second type of animal sacrifice is a concession for compulsive meat eaters. Lower social classes are enjoined to kill a goat in front of goddess Kali on a dark moon night while chanting mantras which explain the sinful reactions of animal killing. The whole purpose is to contain unrestricted meat eating which is so much prevalent in today's slaughterhouse culture. Also by such regulation, a meat eater can be brought back to his senses gradually. He can realize the futility of accruing bad karma just for the sake of some meat. This licensing of animal sacrifice by Vedas is like licensing of liquor by the government. The purpose is not to encourage but to regulate and thereby restrict.

Vedic literatures are replete with stories of Kings who were hunting animals regularly. Again the purpose of such hunting was two fold. First was to contain the menace of violent animals. This allowed the sages to meditate and live peacefully in the forest. They lived there to research, write and pray for the benefit of all living beings.

Secondly, it honed the fighting skills of the ruling class. This enabled them to protect innocent citizens from enemies and antisocial elements.

Strictures Against Animal Killing In World's Religions
Animal Killing And Buddhism

"For the sake of love of purity, let the Bodhisattva refrain from eating flesh, which is born of semen, blood etc. To avoid causing terror to living beings, let the disciple, who is disciplining himself to attain compassion, refrain from eating meat... It is not true that meat is proper food and permissible when the animal was not killed by himself, when he did not order to kill it, when it was not especially meant for him."

"There may be some people in the future who, being under the influence of taste for meat will string together in various ways sophistic arguments to defend meat eating. But meat-eating in any form, in any manner and in any place is unconditionally and once and for all prohibited."

"Meat eating I have not permitted to anyone, I do not permit and will not permit..." *~Lord Buddha, (Lanka vatara Sutra) The Lankavatara Sutra, / Daisez Susuki, London: Routiedge 1932*

"The reason for practicing dhyana and seeking to attain samadhi is to escape from the suffering of life, but in seeking to escape from suffering ourselves why should we inflict it upon others? Unless you can so control your minds that even the thought of brutal unkindness and killing is abhorred, you will never be able to escape from the bondage of the worldly life..."

"After my paranirvana in the last kalpa different ghosts will be encountered everywhere deceiving people and teaching them that they can eat meat and still attain enlightenment.. How can a bhikshu, who hopes to become a deliverer of others, himself be living on the flesh of other sentient beings?" *~Lord Buddha, (Surangama Sutra) A Buddhist Bible, ed. Dwight Godard, New York:Dutton 1952*

"All tremble at violence; all fear death. Putting oneself in the place of another, one should not kill nor cause another to kill." *~Lord Buddha, Dhammapada, 129*

"One who, while seeking happiness, oppresses with violence other living beings who also desire happiness, will not find happiness hereafter." *~Lord Buddha, Dhammapada, 131*

"He who has renounced all violence towards all living beings, weak or strong, who neither kills nor causes others to kill - him I do call a holy man." ~*Lord Buddha, Dhammapada, 405 (Dhammapada by Ven.Sri Acarya Duddharakkhita, Budha Vacana Trust,Bangalore)*

"Anyone familiar with the numerous accounts of the Buddha's extraordinary compassion and reverence for living beings - for example his insistence that his monks strain the water they drink lest they inadvertently cause the death of any microorganisms.

A true follower could never believe that Buddha would be indifferent to the sufferings of domestic animals caused by their slaughter for food" - *A Record of Buddhist Religion, I. Tsing, (Trans. J. Takakusu 1966, pp.30-33)*

"The inhabitants are numerous and happy... Throughout the country the people do not kill any living creature, nor drink intoxicating liquor...they do not keep pigs and fowl, and do not sell live cattle; in the markets there are no butcher shops and no dealers in intoxicating drink... Only the chandalas (lowest caste) are fisherman and hunters who consume flesh meat." ~Famous *4th century Chinese Buddhist traveller Fa-hsien (A Record of Buddhistic Kingdoms, trans.l. James Legge, NY: Dover 195 p 43)*

"I have enforced the laws against killing certain animals and many others. But the greatest progress of Righteousness among men comes from the exhortation in favour of non-injury to life and abstention from killing living things." ~*Pillar Edict of King Ashoka (268-233 BC) The Seventh Pillar Edict, in Sources of Indian Tradition, NY: ColumbiaUniv. 'Press 1958.*

"The eating of meat extinguishes the seed of great compassion" ~Mahaparinirvana *(Mahayana Version)*

The 13th Century Zen Master Doyen, while visiting China, asked this question: "What must the mental attitude and daily activities of a student be when he is engaged in Buddhist Meditation and practice?"

Ju-Ching answered that one of the things he should avoid is eating meat. *-Eihel Dogen, Hokyo-ki:Zen Master, Zen Disciple, Udumbara, A Journal of Zen Master Doyen (1980)*

"The salvation of birds and beasts, oneself included - this is the object of Shakyamuni's religious austerities." *-Zen Master Ikkyu*

"In China and Japan the eating of meat was looked upon as an evil and was ostracized... The eating of meat gradually ceased (around 517) and then tended to become general. It became a matter of course not to use any kind of meat in the meals of temples and monasteries." *-Encyclopaedia of Buddhism, Govt. of Cylon Press (1963)*

The Buddhist emperor Ashoka (304 BC - 232 BC) was a vegetarian and a determined promoter of nonviolence to animals. He promulgated detailed laws aimed at the protection of many species, abolished animal sacrifice at his court, and admonished the population to avoid all kinds of unnecessary killing and injury. Ashoka has asserted protection to fauna, which we could understand from his edicts, "Twenty-six years after my coronation various animals were declared to be protected - parrots, mainas, aruna, ruddy geese, wild ducks, nandimukhas, gelatas, bats, queen ants, terrapins, boneless fish, vedareyaka, gangapuputaka, sankiya fish, tortoises, porcupines, squirrels, deer, bulls, okapinda, wild asses, wild pigeons, domestic pigeons and all four-footed creatures that are neither useful nor edible. Those nanny goats, ewes and sows which are with young or giving milk to their young are protected, and so are young ones less than six months old. Cocks are not to be caponized, husks hiding living beings are not to

When there was too much animal killing, the incarnation of Lord Buddha was there to stop animal killing. In Buddhism there is no animal killing. Although they are now killing animals, but originally Buddha religion means non-violence. Also Lord Christ also said, "Thou shalt not kill." And Krsna says, ahimsa. So in no religion unnecessary killing of animals is allowed. Even in Mohammedans, they are also... Kurvani. Kurvani means they can kill animals in the Mosque. So everywhere animal killing is restricted.
- Srila Prabhupada (Room Conversation with Professor Durckheim, June 19, 1974, Germany)

be burnt and forests are not to be burnt either without reason or to kill creatures. One animal is not to be fed to another."-*Edicts of Ashoka on Fifth Pillar (Encyclopaedia of Religion and Ethics vol. 2 p. 124-125; Spencer p. 85-86; Tähtinen p. 37, 107, 111.)*

"There is just no reason why animals should be slaughtered to serve as human diet when there are so many substitutes. Man can live without meat." -*The Dalai Lama*

Animal Killing And Islam

"...but to hunt...is forbidden you, so long as ye are on the pilgrimage. Be mindful of your duty to Allah, unto Whom you will all be gathered." -*Koran, surah 5, verse 96* (In Mecca, the birthplace of Mohammed, no creature can be slaughtered and that perfect harmony should exist between all living beings. Muslim pilgrims approach Mecca wearing a shroud ('ihram'). From the moment they wear this religious cloth, absolutely no killing is allowed. Mosquitos, lice, grasshoppers, and other living creatures must also be protected. If a pilgrim sees an insect on the ground, he will motion to stop his comrades from accidentally stepping on it.)

"There is not an animal on the earth, nor a flying creature flying on two wings, but they are all peoples like unto you." -*Koran, (surah 6, verse 38)*

"God assigned the earth to all living creatures" -*Koran (Majeed 55:10-12)*

"It behooves you to treat the animals gently." -*Koran (Majeed 4:118-19, 5:103)*

"All creatures are like a family of God; and He loves the most those

Thus it is out of compassion that the Lord appears in His different forms. Lord Sri Krsna appeared on this planet out of compassion for fallen souls; Lord Buddha appeared out of compassion for the poor animals who were being killed by the demons; Lord Nrsimhadeva appeared out of compassion for Prahlada Maharaja. The conclusion is that the Lord is so compassionate upon the fallen souls within this material world that He comes Himself or sends His devotees and His servants to fulfill His desire to have all the fallen souls come back home, back to Godhead.
-*Srila Prabhupada (Srimad Bhagavatam 4.22.42)*

who are the most beneficent to His family." ~Hadith *Mishkat 3:1392*

"Therewith He causes crops to grow for you, and the olive and the date-palm and grapes and all kinds of fruit. Lo! Herein is indeed a portent for people who reflect." ~*Koran, surah 16, verse 11*

"A token unto them is the dead earth. We revive it, and We bring forth from it grain—so that they will eat thereof. And We have placed therein gardens of the date-palm and grapes, and We have caused springs of water to gush forth therein. That they may not eat of the fruit thereof and their hands created it not. Will they not, then, give thanks?" ~*Koran, surah 36, verses 33-35*

"Their flesh will never reach Allah, nor yet their blood - but your devotion and piety will reach Him." ~*Koran (22:37)*

"Eating the meat of a cow causes disease (marz), its milk is health (safa) and its clarified butter (ghee) is medicine (dava)." ~*Ihya Ulum ul-Din, Al-Ghazzali (1058-1111)*

"Neither eat the sea creatures for this is cruel. Nor seek nor desire thy food from the painful slaughtering of animals." ~*Abu l'Ala*

"Maim not the brute beasts" ~*Prophet Mohammed*

Judaism And Christianity

"Thou shall not kill"
~*Sixth Commandment, (Exodus 20:13; Deuteronomy 5:17)*

And God said, "Behold, I have given you every herb bearing seed, which is upon the face of all the earth, and every tree, in which is the fruit of a tree yielding seed; to you it shall be for food. And to every beast of the earth, and to every fowl of the air, and to every thing that creepeth upon the earth, wherein there is a living soul, I have given every green herb for food: and it was so." ~*Genesis 1:29-30*

"The wolf and the lamb will feed together, and the lion will eat straw like the ox, but dust will be the serpent's food. They will neither hunt nor destroy on all my holy mountain," says the Lord. ~*Isaiah 65:25*

God said "What I want is mercy, not sacrifice." ~*Hosea 6:6*

"But flesh with the life thereof, which is the blood thereof, shall ye not eat. And surely your blood of your lives will I require; at the hand of every beast will I require it." ~*Genesis 9.4-5*

"To what purpose is the multitude of your sacrifices unto me? Saith the Lord: I am full of the burnt offerings of rams, and the fat of fed beasts; and I delight not in the blood of bullocks, or of lambs, or of goats. When ye spread forth your hands, I will hide Mine eyes from you: yea, when ye make many prayers, I will not hear, for your hands are full of blood." ~*Isaiah 1.11,15*

"It shall be a perpetual statute for your generations throughout all your dwellings, that ye eat neither fat nor blood. ~*Leviticus 3.17*

And whatsoever man there be of the house of Israel, or of strangers who sojourn among you, that eateth any manner of blood; I will even set My face against that soul that eateth blood." ~*Leviticus 17.10*

"He that killeth an ox is as if he slew a man." ~*Isaiah 66.3*

"God giveth the grains and the fruits of the earth for food: and for righteous man truly there is no other lawful sustenance for the body."
~ *Jesus, The Gospel of the Holy Twelve*

Jesus Ate Meat, Why Shouldn't we?

Another common objection to vegetarianism is, "Jesus Christ ate meat, so why shouldn't we?" But vegetarian Christians point out that the ancient Greek, from which the New Testament was translated, does not support the contention that Christ ate meat. For example, Greek words like brosimos, prosphagion, and trophe, all of which mean simply "food, or "nourishment," were loosely translated as "meat" (except in the New English Bible). And, vegetarian Christians assert, where the Bible states that Christ was offered fish and a honeycomb and accepted 'it' (singular), it means the honeycomb. In the Old Testament a verse predicts this of the youthful Christ: "He shall eat butter and honey, that he may know to refuse the evil and to choose the good." (Isaiah 7:15) The purport would seem to be that to behave otherwise would lead to a brutish mentality, which cannot be accepted in the character of Christ.

In many more places the word 'meat' has been wrongly inserted. For example, in John (4.8) it states: "For his disciples were gone away unto the city to buy meat." The word meat was taken from the Greek word trophe, which actually means nourishment. This is exactly the same case in Acts (9.19): "And when he had received meat, he was strengthened." When translated accurately it means that by receiving nourishment, he felt stronger.

In Luke (8.55) we find, "And her spirit came again and she arose straightaway: and he (Jesus) commanded to give her meat." The word meat in this case was translated from the Greek word phago, which translated correctly simply means to eat.

In I Corinthians (8.8) it states: "But meat commendeth us not to God, for neither, if we eat, are we the better; neither if we eat not, are we the worse." The word for meat here is broma, which actually means food. Therefore, this verse signifies that eating or not eating food has little to do with our relationship to God and not, as some people think, that eating meat holds no wrong.

In Romans (14.20-21) the verses are: "For meat destroy not the word of God. All things indeed are pure; but it is evil for that man who eateth with offence. It is good neither to eat flesh, nor to drink wine, nor anything whereby thy brother stumbleth, or is offended, or is made weak." The word for meat here is broma, which actually means foods, and the word for flesh is kreas, which does mean flesh. Therefore, this verse makes it clear that flesh eating is unacceptable.

If the Bible explains that eating meat is wrong, then what is the

"Lord Christ says 'Thou shalt not kill'; why you are killing?" They give evidence that "Christ also ate meat sometimes." Sometimes Christ ate meat, that's all right, but did Christ say that "You maintain big, big slaughterhouse and go on eating meat?" There is no common sense even. Christ might have eaten. Sometimes he... If there was no, nothing available for eating, what could you do? That is another question. In great necessity, when there is no other food except taking meat... That time is coming. In this age, Kali-yuga, gradually food grains will be reduced. It is stated in the Srimad-Bhagavatam, Twelfth Canto. No rice, no wheat, no milk, no sugar will be available. One has to eat meat. This will be the condition. And maybe to eat the human flesh also. This sinful life is degrading so much so that they will become more and more sinful. - S r i l a *Prabhupada (Lecture, Bhagavad-gita 2.6 — London, August 6, 1973)*

proper thing to eat? Genesis (1.29) clearly states: "And God said, Behold, I have given you every herb bearing seed, which is on the face of all the earth, and every tree, in which is the fruit of a tree yielding seed; to you it shall be for meat." This makes it quite obvious that the food for human beings is herbs, seeds, grains, and fruits.

We also find in Isaiah (7.14-15): "Therefore the Lord Himself shall give you a sign; Behold, a young woman shall conceive, and bear a son, and shall call his name Immanuel. Butter and honey shall he eat, that he may know to refuse the evil, and choose the good." The first verse is often quoted by Christians for proof that Jesus was the savior, but the next verse shows that he will be a vegetarian to know the difference between right and wrong.

Christianity And Animal Killing - A Conversation

The following conversation between His Divine Grace A.C. Bhaktivedanta Swami Prabhupada and Cardinal Jean Danielou took place in Paris on August 9, 1973.

Srila Prabhupada: Jesus Christ said, "Thou shall not kill." So why is it that the Christian people are engaged in animal killing?

Cardinal Danielou: Certainly in Christianity it is forbidden to kill, but we believe that there is a difference between the life of a human being and the life of the beasts. The life of a human being is sacred because man is made in the image of God; therefore, to kill a human being is forbidden.

Srila Prabhupada: But the Bible does not simply say, "Do not kill the human being." It says broadly, "Thou shall not kill."

Cardinal Danielou: We believe that only human life is sacred.

Srila Prabhupada: That is your interpretation. The commandment is "Thou shalt not kill."

Cardinal Danielou: It is necessary for man to kill animals in order to have food to eat.

Srila Prabhupada: No. Man can eat grains, vegetables, fruits, and milk.

Cardinal Danielou: No flesh?

Srila Prabhupada: No. Human beings are meant to eat vegetarian food. The tiger does not come to eat your fruits. His prescribed food is animal flesh. But man's food is vegetables, fruits, grains, and milk products. So how can you say that animal killing is not a sin?

Cardinal Danielou: We believe it is a question of motivation. If the killing of an animal is for giving food to the hungry, then it is justified.

Srila Prabhupada: But consider the cow: we drink her milk; therefore, she is our mother. Do you agree?

Cardinal Danielou: Yes, surely.

Srila Prabhupada: So if the cow is your mother, how can you support killing her? You take the milk from her, and when she's old and cannot give you milk, you cut her throat. Is that a very humane proposal? In India those who are meat eaters are advised to kill some lower animals like goats, pigs, or even buffalo. But cow killing is the greatest sin. In preaching Krishna consciousness we ask people not to eat any kind of meat, and my disciples strictly follow this principle. But if, under certain circumstances, others are obliged to eat meat, then they should eat the flesh of some lower animal. Don't kill cows. It is the greatest sin. And as long as a man is sinful, he cannot understand God. The human being's main business is to understand God and to love Him. But if you remain sinful, you will never be able to understand God -- what to speak of loving Him.

Cardinal Danielou: I think that perhaps this is not an essential point. The important thing is to love God. The practical commandments can vary from one religion to the next.

Srila Prabhupada: So, in the Bible God's practical commandment is that you cannot kill; therefore killing cows is a sin for you.

Cardinal Danielou: God says to the Indians that killing is not good, and he says to the Jews that...

Srila Prabhupada: No, no. Jesus Christ taught, "Thou shall not kill." Why do you interpret this to suit your own convenience?

Cardinal Danielou: But Jesus allowed the sacrifice of the Paschal Lamb.

Srila Prabhupada: But he never maintained a slaughterhouse.

Cardinal Danielou: (laughs) No, but he did eat meat.

Srila Prabhupada: When there is no other food, someone may eat meat in order to keep from starving. That is another thing. But it is most sinful to regularly maintain slaughterhouses just to satisfy your tongue. Actually, you will not even have a human society until this cruel practice of maintaining slaughterhouses is stopped. And although animal killing may sometimes be necessary for survival, at least the mother animal, the cow, should not be killed. That is simply human decency. In the Krsna consciousness movement our practice is that we don't allow the killing of any animals. Krsna says, patram puspam phalam toyam yo me bhaktya prayacchati: "Vegetables, fruits, milk, and grains should be offered to Me in devotion" [Bhagavad-gita 9.16]. We take only the remnants of Krsna's food (prasada). The trees offer us many varieties of fruits, but the trees are not killed. Of course, one living entity is food for another living entity, but that does not mean you can kill your mother for food. Cows are innocent; they give us milk. You take their milk -- and then kill them in the slaughterhouse. This is sinful.

Student: Srila Prabhupada, Christianity's sanction of meat eating is based on the view that lower species of life do not have a soul like the human being's.

Srila Prabhupada: That is foolishness. First of all, we have to understand the evidence of the soul's presence within the body. Then we can see whether the human being has a soul and the cow does not. What are the different characteristics of the cow and the man? If we find a difference in characteristics, then we can say that in the animal there is no soul. But if we see that the animal and the human being have the same characteristics, then how can you say that the animal has no soul? The general symptoms are that the animal eats, you eat; the animal sleeps, you sleep; the animal mates, you mate; the animal defends, and you defend. Where is the difference?

Cardinal Danielou: We admit that in the animal there may be the same type of biological existence as in men, but there is no soul. We believe that the soul is a human soul.

Srila Prabhupada: Our Bhagavad-gita says sarva-yonisu, "In all species of life the soul exists." The body is like a suit of clothes. You have black clothes; I am dressed in saffron clothes. But within the dress you are a human being, and I am also a human being. Similarly, the bodies of the different species are just like different types of dress. There are 8,400,000 species, or dresses, but within each one is a spirit soul, a part and parcel of God. Suppose a man has two sons, not equally meritorious.

"We have enslaved the rest of the animal creation, have treated our distant cousins in fur and feathers so badly that beyond doubt, if they were able to formulate a religion, they would depict the devil in human form."   *-William Ralph Inge.*

29

One may be a Supreme Court judge and the other may be a common laborer, but the father claims both as his sons. He does not make the distinction that the son who is a judge is very important, and the worker son is not important. And if the judge son says, "My dear father, your other son is useless; let me cut him up and eat him," will the father allow this?

Cardinal Danielou: Certainly not, but the idea that all life is part of the life of God is difficult for us to admit. There is a great difference between human life and animal life.

Srila Prabhupada: That difference is due to the development of consciousness. In the human body there is developed consciousness. Even a tree has a soul, but a tree's consciousness is not very developed. If you cut a tree it does not resist. Actually, it does resist, but only to a very small degree. There is a scientist named Jagadish Chandra Bose who has made a machine which shows that trees and plants are able to feel pain when they are cut. And we can see directly that when someone comes to kill an animal, it resists, it cries, it makes a horrible sound. So it is a matter of the development of consciousness. But the soul is there within all living beings.

Cardinal Danielou: But metaphysically, the life of man is sacred. Human beings think on a higher platform than the animals do.

Srila Prabhupada: What is that higher platform? The animal eats to maintain his body, and you also eat in order to maintain your body. The cow eats grass in the field, and the human being eats meat from a huge slaughterhouse full of modern machines. But just because you have big machines and a ghastly scene, while the animal simply eats grass, this does not mean that you are so advanced that only within your body is there a soul, and that there is not a soul within the body of the animal. That is illogical. We can see that the basic characteristics are the same in the animal and the human being.

Cardinal Danielou: But only in human beings do we find a metaphysical search for the meaning of life.

Srila Prabhupada: Yes. So metaphysically search out why you believe that there is no soul within the animal -- that is metaphysics. If you are thinking metaphysically, that's all right. But if you are thinking like an animal, then what is the use of your metaphysical study? "Metaphysical" means "above the physical" or, in other words, "spiritual." In the Bhagavad-gita Krsna says, sarva-yonisu kaunteya: "In every living being there is a spirit soul." That is metaphysical understanding. Now either you accept Krsna's teachings as metaphysical, or you'll have to take a third-class fool's opinion as metaphysical. Which do you accept?

Cardinal Danielou: But why does God create some animals who eat other animals? There is a fault in the creation, it seems.

Srila Prabhupada: It is not a fault. God is very kind. If you want to eat animals, then He'll give you full facility. God will give you the body of a tiger in your next life so that you can eat flesh very freely. "Why are you maintaining slaughterhouses? I'll give you fangs and claws. Now eat." So the meat eaters are awaiting such punishment. The animal eaters become tigers, wolves, cats, and dogs in their next life -- to get more facility.

(Copyrights BBT International)

Humanity Turning Into Walking Graves

Meat eating is similar to consigning a corpse to an earthly grave. Both entail burying a dead body, in the belly in the first case and in the ground in the other. Only difference is that one grave is stationary and the other is mobile.

George Bernard Shaw rightly puts this in his famous poem:
We are the living graves of murdered beasts,

So this is nature's law. You don't require to be sent to the slaughterhouse. You'll make your slaughterhouse at home. You'll kill your own child. Abortion. This is nature's law. ....If you kill, you must be killed.
Bhagavan: They kill the cow, which is a mother, and then sometimes they get, when their mother kills them.
-Srila Prabhupada (Room Conversation -- June 11, 1974, Paris)

Slaughtered to satisfy our appetites.
We never pause to wonder at our feasts,
If animals like men could possibly have rights.
We pray on Sunday that we may have light,
To guide our footsteps on the paths we tread.
We are sick of war, we do not want to fight,
The thought of it now fills our hearts with dread,
And yet we gorge ourselves upon the dead.
Like carrion crows we live and feed on meat,
Regardless of the suffering and pain
We cause by doing so.
If thus we treat
Defenseless animals for sport or gain,
How can we hope in this world to attain
The Peace we say we are anxious for?
Thus cruelty begets its offspring—War.

There is an alarming rise in global meat consumption. As per Food and Agriculture Organization of the United Nations (FAO) statistical

database, since 1960 global meat consumption has more than trebled. This is attributed partly to the increase in affluence in many countries. A joint IFPRI/FAO/ILRI study suggested that global production and consumption of meat will continue to rise, from 233 million metric tons (Mt) in the year 2000 to 300 million Mt in 2020.

The consumption of poultry meat has increased from 9 million Mt in 1960, to 15 in 1970, 26 in 1980, 41 in 1990 and 68 million Mt in 2000, thereby overtaking the production of beef (60 million Mt in 2000). Consumption of meat in the U.S. is 124 kg/capita/year, compared to the global average of 38 kg. The countries that consume the least amount of meat are in Africa and South Asia.

But What About Killing Plants?

One of the strongest objections animal killers raise against vegetarianism is that vegetarians still have to kill plants, and that this

Formerly if somebody is attacked by another man, many persons will come to help him: "Why this man is attacked?" But at the present moment if one man is attacked, the passersby will not care for it because they have lost their sympathy or mercifulness for others. Our neighbor may starve, but we don't care for it. But formerly the sympathy for other living entities, even for an ant... Just like Maharaja Pariksit, while he was touring on his kingdom, he saw that one man was trying to kill a cow. Pariksit Maharaja saw. Immediately he took his sword that "Who are you? You are killing a cow in my kingdom?" Because the king is supposed, or the government is supposed to give everyone protection, not that the government is meant for giving protection to the human being and not to the animals. Because it is Kali-yuga, the government discriminates between two nationals. National means one who has taken birth in the land. That is called national. That is... You know, everyone. So the trees, they are also born in the land, the aquatics also born in the land. The flies, the reptiles, the snakes, the birds, the beasts, human beings -- everyone is born in that land. Suppose your land, America, United States... Why the government should give protection to one class of living entities, rejecting others? This means they have lost their sympathy for others. - Srila Prabhupada (Lecture, New Vrindaban, September 2, 1972)

33

is also violence. But there is no logic in equating fully sentient animals like cows with lowly vegetables. Certainly, plants are as alive as cows; modern experiments prove that plants have feelings, and the Bhagavad-gita, the essence of all Vedic teachings, confirms that all life forms contain spirit souls qualitatively equal to one another.

Still all killings are not the same. Going by the argument, killing the person so arguing and killing a potato should be the same but he would not agree to that. Besides most of the time the plants are not killed. At the time of harvesting, the rice or wheat stalks turn yellow and are already dead. When plucking an apple or tomato, the plant is not killed. Whatever violence exists in vegetarian diet, it is minimal because plants have been put by nature in a kind of anaesthesia. That is why chopping a potato and killing a cow creates very different scenes. Potato does not scream, writhe or tries to flee away. Is it the same thing to operate a person who is fully conscious and a person with anaesthesia?

We have to eat something, and the Vedas also say, jivo jivasya jivanam: one living entity is food for another. So from a humane standpoint, the problem in choosing a diet is not how to avoid killing altogether—an impossible proposal—but *how to cause the least suffering* while meeting the nutritional needs of the body. A well-balanced diet of fruits, grains, vegetables, and milk products meets these criteria, and this diet is recommended in such scriptures as the Bhagavad-gita as most truly human.

Legalized Terrorism - Animal Abuse And Killing

Barely a few years into it, the twenty-first century is already clearly marked as the "Age of Terrorism." The attacks of September 11, 2001 marked a salient turning point in the history of the U.S. and indeed of global geopolitics. The U.S. declared its number one priority to be the "War on Terrorism," and its domestic, national, and international policies have changed accordingly. In his address to the nation shortly after the 9/11 attacks, Bush used the terms "terror," "terrorism," and "terrorist" thirty-two times without ever defining what he meant.

In the amorphous name of "terrorism," wars are being fought, geopolitical dynamics are shifting, the U.S. is aggressively reasserting its traditional imperialist role as it defies international law and world bodies, and the state is sacrificing liberties to "security." One of the most commonly used words in the current vocabulary, "terrorism" is also one of the most abused terms. Steve Best defines terrorism "as any intentional act to injure or kill a living, sentient, innocent being for scientific, political or economic purposes." This is a sane, sensible and rational definition. Going by this definition, there are lot more terrorists in the world than those on FBI's list. Practically every one fits as a terrorist in this definition.

Animals which are captured, enslaved, tortured and slaughtered are being "terrorized". Indeed animals are sentient - when they scream in labs, when they suffer in rodeos and when they stand before the butcher... they are all in terror of our brutal power over them.

Real Terrorism

In this way, not all terrorists fight with guns and bombs, and not all terrorists fight strictly for political gain. There are men and women in this world who are terrorists in another real sense.

Virtually all definitions of terrorism, even by "progressive" human rights champions, outright banish from consideration the most excessive violence of all—that which the human species unleashes against all nonhuman species. Speciesism is so ingrained and entrenched in the human mind that the human mass murder of animals does not even appear on the conceptual radar screen. Any attempt to perceive nonhuman animals as innocent victims of violence and human animals as terrorists is rejected with derision.

Nations As Terrorist States

But if terrorism is linked to intentional violence inflicted on innocent persons for ideological, political, or economic motivations, and nonhuman animals also are "persons"—subjects of a life—then the human war against animals is terrorism. Every individual who terrifies, injures, tortures, and/or kills an animal is a terrorist; fur farms, factory farms, foie gras, vivisection, and other exploitative operations are terrorist industries; and governments that support these industries are terrorist states. The true weapons of mass destruction are the gases, rifles, stun guns, cutting blades, and forks and knives used to experiment on, kill, dismember, and consume animal bodies.

The anti-terror crusader, US alone kills more than one million animals per hour which are cruelly raised, handled, transported, stocked and killed.

Each year in USA alone,

• Over 10 billion farmed animals are killed for food consumption (which translates to over 1 million animals per hour);

• 17–70 million animals are killed for testing and experimentation;

• Over 100 million are killed for hunting; and

• 7–8 million animals are trapped or raised in confinement for their fur.

Mahatma Gandhi was right when he said, "the greatness of a nation is judged by the way it treats its animals".

This crime against creation will never go unpunished. Ordinary laws can be circumvented and courts can be bribed but no one can escape the stringent laws of material nature. Unnecessary killing of

even an ant is a serious crime.

It is just a question of time before we pay through our nose for all this mischief. The mills of God grind slowly, but they grind exceeding fine.

Section-II

Why Is Cow Considered Sacred In India?

"It may indeed be doubted whether butchers' meat is anywhere a necessary of life. Grain and other vegetables, with the help of milk, cheese, and butter, or oil where butter is not to be had, it is known from experience, can, without any butchers' meat, afford the most plentiful, the most wholesome, the most nourishing, and the most invigorating diet. Decency nowhere requires that any man should eat butchers' meat."
-Adam Smith (The Wealth of Nations)

1.

Sacred Cow

A Dumb Indian Idea?

When used in a modern sense, the term holy cow or sacred cow sums up the idiosyncrasies, superstitions, folklores and primitive obstinacies of a backward India. The average Westerner (or a person with that mindset) finds this highly amusing that Indians 'worship' cows. Time and again in last two hundred years, this fact has been brought up, much to the astonishment of giggling school girls in London and Newyork. And this idea has found plenty of takers in all parts of the world, including India with the spread of Western values and ideologies.

On the other hand, hamburgers and Mcdonald's are the icons of a chic and smart world. They represent a world which has wriggled itself out from the fetters of primitiveness and blind belief.

Just as Britney and Madonna are female icons, Marlboro Man and Rambo are the male ideal, cows are our food, nothing more. From Cleveland to Cairo to Caracas, Baywatch is entertainment and CNN is news...and cows are the food. And you got to be dumb if you suggest anything to the contrary.

These are the times of homogenization. We are living in a world in which people everywhere are eating the same food, Mcdonald and KFC, wearing the same clothing, jeans and T-shirt and live in houses built from the same materials. Anywhere you go you find multi-lane highways, concrete cities, a cultural landscape featuring grey business suits, fast food chains, Hollywood films, and cellular phones. It is a world in which every society employs the same technologies, depends on the same centrally managed economy, offers the same Western education for its children, speaks the same language, consumes the same media images, holds the same values, and even thinks the same thoughts and carry the same idea ....Cows are simply dumb animals and they taste good.

The world over, the term "sacred cow" has come to mean any stubborn loyalty to a long-standing institution which impedes natural progress. The term originates in India, where the cow is said to be literally worshiped. The common, popular view of India in the West is that of an underdeveloped nation steeped in superstitions. Overpopulated, overcrowded, undereducated, and bereft of most modern amenities, India is seen to be a backward nation in many respects by the 'progressive' West. "If only India would abandon her old wives' tales and eat cow!" Over several decades many attempts have been made by the compassionate West to alleviate India's burden of poor logic, and to replace it with rational thinking.

Much of the religious West finds common ground with the rationalists, with whom they otherwise are usually at odds, on the issue of India's "sacred cow." Indeed, worshiping God is one thing, but to worship the cow is a theological outlook much in need of reevaluation. Man is said to have dominion over the animals, but it would appear that the Indians have it backwards.

In an age when we pay to kill our own children in the womb, its no surprise that Indians are mocked for honoring the cow.

The central fact of Hinduism is cow protection. Cow protection to me is one of the most wonderful phenomenon in human evolution. It takes the human being beyond his species. The cow to me means the entire subhuman world. Man through the cow is enjoined to realize his identity with all that lives....Protection of the cow means the protection of the whole dumb creation of God....Cow protection is the gift of Hinduism to the world. And Hinduism will live as long as there are Hindus to protect the cow. Hindus will be judged not by their tilaks, not by the correct chanting of mantras, not by their pilgrimages, not by their most punctilious observance of caste rules but by their ability to protect the cow ~ Mahatma Gandhi

Were The Indians Dumb? Are The Modern Dudes Really Smart?

The term sacred cow finds its origin in the ancient Vedic tradition, dating back to thousands of years. What really prompted these folks to revere and worship the cows? Were they really so stupid as to worship an animal? Are we really that smart now to ridicule their idea? Why didn't they propose to worship any other animal like tiger, dog or monkey. Take a look at the following facts about these folks.

Native tongue of the ancient Indians was Sanskrit. British scholar Sir Willian Jones considers it to be the mother of all European Languages including Latin. Sanskrit is the world's oldest known tongue and Nasa has declared it to be "the only unambiguous language on the planet". Many scholars have established presence of words in European Languages that have come out of Sanskrit.

It is the most systematic language in the world. The vastness and the versatility, and power of expression can be appreciated by the fact that this language has 65 words to describe various forms of earth, 67 words for water, and over 250 words to describe rainfall.

The Sanskrit verbal adjective samskrta- may be translated as "well or completely formed; refined, adorned, highly elaborated" The corpus of Sanskrit literature encompasses a rich tradition of poetry and drama as well as scientific, technical, philosophical and dharma texts. Sanskrit continues to be widely used as a ceremonial language in Hindu religious rituals and Buddhist practice in the forms of hymns and mantras.

Just to learn Sanskrit grammar properly, it takes a minimum of 12 years. European scholarship in Sanskrit, begun by Heinrich Roth(1620-1668) and Johann Ernst Hanxleden (1681-1731), is regarded as responsible for the discovery of the Indo-European language family by Sir William Jones. This scholarship played an important role in the development of Western philology, or historical linguistics. Sir William Jones, speaking to The Asiatic Society in Calcutta on February 2, 1786, said:

"The Sanskrit language, whatever be its antiquity, is of a wonderful structure; more perfect than the Greek, more copious than the Latin, and more exquisitely refined than either, yet bearing to both of them a stronger affinity, both in the roots of verbs and in the forms of grammar, than could possibly have been produced by accident."

Throughtout the length and breadth of India, even a commoner could speak and write in Sanskrit. Practically the whole subcontinent was literate because the education, unlike today, was imparted by selfless brahmanas on village level.

Written tradition in Sanskrit is 5000 years old. Before that there was no need for written word. The brains were so sharp that all the knowledge existed in oral tradition. A student could memorize everything simply by hearing it once from the teacher. All these super brains were subsisting on the super foods – cow's milk and butter, added with some grains and fruits. The cows greatly outnumbered humans.

It was not just the language. Science and technology in ancient India covered all major branches of knowledge like mathematics, astronomy, physics, chemistry, medical science, surgery, fine arts, mechanical and production technology, civil engineering, architecture, shipbuilding and navigation, sports and games etc.

Ancient India was a land of saintly scholars and scientists. India's contribution to science and technology include:

Mathematics - In India, mathematics has its roots in Vedic literatures which are nearly 5000 years old. Apart from original vedic texts, between 1000 BC and 1000 AD various treatises on mathematics were authored. In these treatises were set forth, for the first time, the concept of zero, the techniques of algebra and algorithm, square root and cube root. A method of graduated calculation was documented in the Pancha-Siddhantika (Five Principles) in the 5th Century, long before Newton and Leibniz. The technique is said to be dating from Vedic times circa 3000 B.C. Geometry called Rekha-ganita in ancient India was formulated and applied in the drafting of Mandalas for architectural purposes. They were also displayed in the geometric patterns used in many temple motifs.

Astronomy - Astronomy literally means, "the law of the stars" and refers to the science involving the observation and explanation of events occurring beyond the Earth and its atmosphere. Ancient India's contributions in the field of astronomy are well known and well documented. The earliest references to astronomy are found in the Rig Veda, dating back to 3000 BC. By 500 AD, ancient Indian

Formerly, any big man, any big scholar, they would be big scholar in Sanskrit. Sanskrit was the written language. Even in the beginning of the British period, Sanskrit was written language. It is the policy of Lord McCauley that he transformed the whole attitude. They made a plan that "If Indians remain as Indian, then we cannot rule over. Then we cannot rule over. We must make them Anglicized." So that policy was followed for two hundred years, so India has lost its original culture. -Srila Prabhupada (Lecture on Maha-mantra, New York, September 8, 1966)

astronomy had emerged as an important part of Indian studies and its affect is also seen in several treatises of that period. In some instances, astronomical principles were borrowed to explain matters pertaining to astrology, like casting of a horoscope. Apart from this linkage of astronomy with astrology in ancient India, science of astronomy continued to develop independently, and culminated into original findings like:

-The calculation of occurrences of eclipses

-Determination of the circumferences and sizes of the planets. (They knew long ago that Earth is round. Planets were described by the words like 'bhugola' or 'brahmanda', meaning a round or egg-like shape.)

-The theory of gravitation

-Structure of the universe.

Physics - Physics of ancient India, like mathematics and astronomy, is replete with theories and calculations that anticipate western scientific achievements by many centuries.

These treatises included the concepts of atom (Anu, Parmanu), theory of relativity (Sapekshavada), creation of the cosmos, constituents of matter, mysteries of the universe, laws of motion etc. These ideas were of fundamental import and had been developed in India independently and prior to the development of ideas in the Greco-Roman world.

6th century BC physicists, Kanada and Katyayana are well knows for their pioneering work on the atomic theory and atomic constitution of the material world. They considered atom to be indivisible and indestructible. Speaking of ancient Indian expositions, A.L. Basham, the veteran Australian Indologist says, "They were brilliant imaginative explanations of the physical structure of the world, and in a large measure, agree with the discoveries of modern physics."

Chemistry - The advanced nature of ancient India's chemical science finds expression in fields like distillation of perfumes and fragrant ointments, manufacturing of dyes and chemicals, polishing of mirrors, preparation of pigments and colours etc. Paintings found on walls of Ajanta and Ellora (both World heritage sites) look fresh even after 1000 years. This feat can not be achieved with the available technology today.

Also they were very advanced in metallurgy. By the side of Qutub Minar in Delhi stands an Iron Pillar which is believed to be cast in the Gupta period around 500 AD. The pillar is 7.32 meters tall, tapering from a diameter of 40 cm at the base to 30 cm at the top and is estimated to weigh 6 tonnes. It has been standing in the open for last 1500 years, withstanding the wind, heat and weather, but still has not rusted, except some minor natural erosion. This is a miracle even when compared with metallurgical achievements of the 20th century.

Medical Science & Surgery - Ayurveda as a science of medicine owes its origins in ancient India and it literally means 'the science of life or longevity'. Ayurveda constitutes ideas about ailments and diseases, their symptoms, diagnosis and cure, and relies heavily on herbal medicines, including extracts of several plants.

Ancient scholars of India like Atreya, and Agnivesa have dealt with principles of Ayurveda as long back as 800 BC. Their works and other developments were consolidated by Charaka who compiled a compendium of Ayurvedic principles and practices in his treatise Charaka-Samhita. This has remained a standard textbook for almost 2000 years and has been translated into many languages, including Arabic and Latin. Charaka-samhita deals with a variety of matters covering physiology, etiology and embryology, concepts of digestion,

So India lost its culture, educated persons they lost. And the mass of people, they were not educated. They have not lost, but they don't find any good example by the leaders. They are simply staying somehow or other in their original culture, but there is no encouragement by the leaders.....Discovery of India; 'For so long India was not discovered' -- by opiate or something like, as the Russians say -- 'Now it is discovered.' And that its leaders have to become Anglicized or Europeanized-industry, the Western way of living, eating, and everything. Pollution, everything. Otherwise, we have seen in our childhood how happy people were. Simple. If one has five rupees income per month he's happy. I've seen it. Husband, wife, a small family. If he has got five rupees income, they can maintain very nicely, happily."
-Srila Prabhupada (Transcendental Diary, Sri Vrndavana-dhama)

metabolism, and immunity. Preliminary concepts of genetics also find a mention there.

Shushruta, a medical theoretician and practitioner, lived around the same time in the ancient Indian city of Kasi. He wrote a medical compendium called Shushruta-Samhita. This ancient medical compendium describes at least seven branches of surgery: excision, scarification, puncturing, exploration, extraction, evacuation, and suturing. The compendium also deals with matters like rhinoplasty (plastic surgery) and ophthalmology (ejection of cataracts). It also has instructions on studying the human anatomy by using a cadaver. There are thousands of other works on traditional medicine, both in Sanskrit and other vernaculars like Tamil and Malayalam.

Fine Arts - Fine arts permeated the very fabric of people's lives. In Vedic sastras, we find description of innumerable arts out of which sixty four find prominence.

Following are some of the performing and fine arts for which vast resources and references are still available.

Music, instrumental music, dance, drama, painting, body decoration, ornamental arts, cooking, engineering, horticulture, magical entertainment, astrology, gambling, amusements, literature, physical and social arts, erotica etc.

Then there was the art of reciting vedic hymns. It was governed by a fine science of sound and phonetics.

Mechanical & Production Technology - Mechanical and production technology of ancient India ensured processing of natural produce and their conversion into merchandise for trade, commerce and export. A number of travelers and historians (including

India at the present moment, they have lost their culture. In India, five thousand years ago, when Maharaja Pariksit was there, one black man was trying to kill a cow. He immediately took his sword, the king. So "Who are you? You are killing cow in my kingdom?" The same India, the government is sanctioning ten thousand cows to be killed daily. So India is not the same India. India has lost its culture.
~Srila Prabhupada (Room Conversation, London, August 24, 1973)

Megasthanes, Ptolemy, Faxian, Xuanzang, Marco Polo, Al Baruni and Ibn Batuta) have mentioned a variety of items, which were produced, consumed and exported around the world by the ancient Indians. Greek historians have testified to smelting of certain metals in India in the 4th century BC.

Civil engineering & Architecture - In ancient India, architecture and civil engineering was known as sthapatya-kala and it found its expression in construction of temples, palaces and forts across the Indian peninsula and the neighbouring regions. During the periods of Kushan and Maurya empires, the Indian architecture and civil engineering reached the regions like Baluchistan and Afghanistan. Over a period of time, ancient Indian art of construction blended with Greek styles and spread to Central Asia.

On the other side, Indian architecture and civil engineering spread to countries like Sri Lanka, Indonesia, Malaysia, Vietnam, Laos, Cambodia, Thailand, Burma, China, Korea and Japan. Angkor Wat is a living testimony to the contribution of Indian civil engineering and architecture to the Cambodian Khmer heritage.

In mainland India today, there are several architectural marvels including world heritage sites like Ajanta, Ellora, Khajuraho, Mahabodhi Temple, Sanchi, Brihadisvara Temple, Puri, Konark, Mahabalipuram etc.

Shipbuilding & Navigation - Sanskrit and Pali texts have several references to maritime activity by the ancient Indians. The science of

shipbuilding and navigation was well known. They were having trade relations with several countries of across bay of Bengal like Cambodia, Java, Sumatra, Borneo, right up to China and Japan. Similar maritime and trade relations existed with countries across the Arabian Sea like Arabia, Egypt and Persia. America had not been discovered and Europe was not civilized enough to have trade relations with.

Even around circa 500 AD, sextants and mariner's compass were known to Indian shipbuilders and navigators. According to a report published in the Bombay Gazetteer by J.L. Reid, a member of the Institute of Naval Architects and Shipbuilders, England, "The early Hindu astrologers are said to have used the magnet, in fixing the North and East, in laying foundations, and other religious ceremonies. The Hindu compass was an iron fish that floated in a vessel of oil and pointed to the North. The fact of this older Hindu compass seems placed beyond doubt by the Sanskrit word 'Maccha-Yantra', or 'fish-machine', which Molesworth gives as a name for the mariner's compass".

Dumbing Down of The Modern World

After examining vedic culture where cows were protected, we can examine as to what is happening to a cow eating civilization.

In the last few years, startling surveys have come out, exposing the intellectual state of younger generation in the developed countries. While the younger generation in America, Europe and Australia are busy reveling in drug and sex, companies are forced to outsource work to countries in Asia and elsewhere. Many Americans and Australians are finding Indians and other Asians moving in their neighborhood and taking up jobs as doctors, engineers, dentists and scientists.

In a 2007 survey by the British author Hilary Spurling, it was

"Flesh eating is unprovoked murder"
~ Benjamin Franklin

found that a significant percentage of university students in Britain could not write properly or spell or present an argument. No, these weren't university rejects, but students at prestigious establishments.

Prize-winning biographer Hilary Spurling says, "Most contemporary British students arriving at university lack the basic ability to express themselves in writing." The poet and playwright Michelene Wandor says: "They don't know what a sentence is, what a verb is, what a noun is. They struggle with apostrophes and they often don't know what tense they're writing in."

The childrens author Yvonne Coppard agrees. "Their syntax and grammar are sloppy, they have sentences that draggle all over the place, you can see whole pages without paragraphs, and as for speech punctuation - I don't know what happened to that!"

Educationists are blowing the whistle on the scandal of a generation that lacks the basic skills to study for a degree.

University students can't write decent English. Worse, their attempts to do so show that many can't follow a logical train of thought or present a reasoned argument. In fact, growing numbers are not ready for the demands of higher education.

Standards of spelling among university students are now so bad that lecturers are being urged to turn a blind eye to mistakes.

In another survey in US, 50% of 17 year old students in San Francisco did not know where the Pacific Ocean was. A significant percentage of students of the 'New York Institute of Technology', or NYIT for short, could not spell New York. It is pertinent to note that In 1993, 90 million Americans lacked basic literacy.

In another survey, it was found that many British GCSE students could not spell simple words such as 'was' and were writing it as 'whas'. Simple words such as "looked", "there" and "was" were all spelt wrongly in the English GCSE exam scripts. It was brought to noticed when researchers were going through the scripts for Cambridge assessment.

Many undergraduates misspell basic words such as "their", "speech" or even "Wednesday" in essays. First year students were the worst offenders, despite already spending at least 13 years in the education system.

Moving on to Australia, Two-thirds of Australian adults could not spell the word 'embarrass' in a 2009 survey.

The Galaxy survey commissioned by Westpac was conducted on 400 people, aged over 16 years, from Sydney and Melbourne. It showed about 70 per cent could not spell the world 'accommodation'. One in two people wrongly spelt 'accessory', and a quarter had trouble with 'February'.

"Universities are even finding they have masters-level students who cannot spell," says Jack Bovill, Chairman of The Spelling Society. It is not just a question of spelling but overall intellectual capacity is coming down rapidly.

Cows Were Eaten In Ancient India - A Mischievous Propaganda

According to Thomas R. Trautmann, after the 18th-century wave of "Indomania", i.e. enthusiasm for Indian culture and for Sanskrit, as exemplified in the positions of Orientalist scholars such as Sir William Jones, a certain hostility to Sanskrit and to Indian culture in general began to assert itself in Britain in the early 19th century. The hostility was manifest by a neglect of Sanskrit in British academia, as compared to other European countries, and was part of a general push in favor of the idea that India should be culturally, religiously and linguistically assimilated to Britain as far as possible. Traufmann considers that this British hostility to Sanskrit had two separate and logically opposite sources: one was "British Indophobia", which he calls essentially a developmentalist, progressivist, liberal, and non-racial-essentialist critique of Hindu civilization as an aid for the improvement of India along European lines. The other was race science, which was a theorisation of the English "common-sense view" that Indians constituted a "separate, inferior and unimprovable race".

As part of this 'Indophobia', by 1860 the British scholarship started a new school of vedic interpretation. According to it, the Vedas and allied texts advocate cow eating and beef was part of a Vedic diet. Its purpose was to culturally subjugate India and create a whole new class of educated Indians who were brown outside but white inside. They even bribed scholars to write books in support of cow slaughter.

This mischievous propaganda had profound influence on traditional cow culture of India. It had a devastating impact on socio-economic and environmental fronts. British had no compunction in devastating a nation. And they did so quite effectively by abolishing India's centuries old cow culture.

Of all beings the cows in India were considered most sacred. There is not a single passage in the entire vedic literatures which recommends beef eating. On the other hand, in support of cow protection, millions

> *They bribed one Mukerjee, Radha-kunda Mukerjee, doctor, to write book where he has supported cow slaughter. He was given a post, made a parliament member first of all. So this poor man, five hundred rupees per month, he accepted. Then he induced that "You take more money, write like this." So if you pay money... British government's whole policy was that if the Indians are kept strict Hindus, it is next to impossible to govern them. So therefore they adopted this policy. They changed the whole policy how the Hindu will think everything mentioned in the sastra is nonsense.*
> *–Srila Prabhupada (Room Conversation, March 12, 1972, Vrndavana)*

of verses can be quoted. Wherefrom people get the idea that cows were eaten during Vedic times is a mystery to us.

Claim that cows were killed in vedic sacrifices is unfounded. Cows and bulls were used in sacrifices but the purpose was rejuvenation and testing of mantras, not taking their life. An old cow or bull would be sacrificed in a painless process and they would come out young from the sacrificial fire. Priests took life because they were capable of awarding a better life. This ceremony was called 'gomedha yajna'. Today we take life without any capability to give life and therefore all yajnas involving animals are prohibited. The following verse makes it clear:

asvamedham gavalambham

sannyasam pala-paitrkam

devarena sutotpattim

kalau panca vivarjayet

'In this Age of Kali, five acts are forbidden: the offering of a horse in sacrifice, the offering of a cow in sacrifice, the acceptance of the order of sannyasa, the offering of oblations of flesh to the forefathers, and a man's begetting children in his brother's wife.' (Brahma-vaivarta Purana, Krsna-janma-khanda 185.180)

Cow is described in Vedas as aghnya or one who can not be harmed under any circumstances. What to speak of killing, even hurting a

Cow protection is the gift of Hinduism to the world.
~ Gandhi

cow attracted capital punishment. First canto of Srimad Bhagavatam describes how King Pariksit almost killed a rogue who was trying to hurt a cow and bull.

In modern India, supporters of cow slaughter often quote Swami Vivekananda to support their cause. We strongly disagree with the following contention: "You have always to remember that because a little social custom is going to be changed, you are not going to lose your religion, not at all. Remember these customs have already been changed. There was a time in this very India when, without eating beef, no Brahmin could remain a Brahmin ; you read in the Vedas how, when a sanyasin, a king, or a great man came into a house, the best bullock was killed, how in time it was found that as we were an agricultural race, killing the best bulls meant annihilation of the race. Therefore, the practice was stopped, and a voice was raised against the killing of cows... (From Swami Vivekananda's reply to the welcome address at Madurai in 1897, Lectures from Colombo to Almora, Advaita Ashram)

Following prayer to cows in Vedas reflect the attitude of vedic society towards cows:

namaste jayamanaye jataya uta te namah
balebhyah saphebhyo rupayaghnye te namah

O mother cow, you deserve all protection, I offer my obeisances while you appear and after you appear in this world. I offer my respects to your sacred body, to hairs on your body and to your hooves also.

Cow Killing And Abuse - A Byproduct of Industrialization

Srila Prabhupada explains as to what lies at the root of cow slaughter, "So Maharaja Yudhisthira was so pious that during his reign time,

Alas, what wickedness to swallow flesh into our own flesh, to fatten our greedy bodies by cramming in other bodies, to have one living creature fed by the death of another! In the midst of such wealth as earth, the best of mothers, provides, nothing forsooth satisfies you, but to behave like the Cyclopes, inflicting sorry wounds with cruel teeth! You cannot appease the hungry cravings of your wicked, gluttonous stomachs except by destroying some other life. - Pythagoras kamam vavarsa parjanyah [SB 1.10.4]. There was regular rainfall and everything was produced nicely. Sarva-kama-dugha mahi. Sarva-kama. The, another side is that you don't require industries, trade. You don't require. If you have got land and cow, then everything is complete. This is basic principle of Vedic civilization. Have some land. Have some cows. Dhanyena dhanavan gavayah dhanavan. Not industry. There is no need of industry. Because you want some food, nice food, nice milk, nice fruit, that will be produced by nature. You cannot manufacture all these things in the factory. So therefore the..., at the present moment, the big, big factories, they are the activities of the asuras, ugra-karma. All the people are dragged in the city, industrial area, to engage them in the produce of iron bars, big, big iron bars, iron industry, and so many other industries. Capitalists, they have drawn all the innocent people from the village. And they think that "We are getting fat salary." But what is the use of fat salary? One side you get fat salary; another side you have to purchase three rupees a kilo rice. Finish your salary. This is going on. Let them produce their own food. Let him have some land. Let him produce his own food. Let there be cows. Let cows become happy." (Lecture on Srimad-Bhagavatam 1.10.4, Mayapura, June 19, 1973)

Mad Human Beings, Not Mad Cows

Madness is a human trait and hasn't spread to cows yet.

The term 'mad cow' in fact refers to mad human beings who feed grass eating cows a cannibalistic diet of slaughterhouse waste products. In other words, cows are killed and fed to the cows and then she is called 'mad'. Who is really mad in this case?

Syamasundara: These evolutionists, they consider... They don't think there is a soul. They think that the cow is an organism, and we are just more advanced organisms. So we have the right to slaughter the cow because we are more advanced.

Prabhupada: Now, tiger is more advanced. He has the right to kill you. Why you say you are advanced? Why you are claiming that you are advanced? When a tiger is there, he kills you and eats you. He is more advanced. (Philosophical Discussion)

In 1990s, millions of cows were killed in Europe, supposedly to prevent the spread of bovine spongiform encephalopathy, or BSE, an infection affecting cows due to feeding them meat and bone meals.

The Height of Madness - Mass Culling

Mass killing has been a troubleshooting tool in the hands of Western powers. Think of the Americans' plan for getting rid of almost everyone in North Vietnam. Shoot and bomb them until there are so few left that people think the problem has been solved. This philosophy was reflected in the attitude of Boris Yeltsin to the population of Chechnya. Same with Hitler's final solution for getting rid of the Jews and Stalin's final solution for getting rid of all small farmers in Russia. Same with the British in their colonies in Asia and Africa. Just kill and kill and kill!

Whether its Afghanistan or Iraq, if you gonna solve a problem, just kill'em all. In Afghanistan, when Russian generals wanted to clear a minefield, they set the Russian infantry walking through it. They lost a lot of soldiers, but it certainly cleared the minefield.

No regard for life whatsoever. But the killers are unaware of the dire consequences awaiting them. Law of karma exacts more interest than any bank in the world.

2.

Cow Gives And Gives And Gives

In Life And Death, Cow Is A Symbol Of Selfless Service

And now the question: why is cow considered sacred in India? Why is cow given a special place among all living beings. These chapters will address this point.

Who Is The Greatest Giver On Planet Today?

Do we ever pause to ask a question as to who is the greatest giver on planet earth today? What do we see on every table? In every country of the world, breakfast, lunch and dinner? Whether for vegetarians or non-vegetarians, civilized or uncivilized. It is the cow.

The generous cow gives milk, cream, yogurt, cheese, butter and ice cream. Can we imagine life without these valuable products. To the ungrateful meat eaters, she offers sirloin, ribs, rump, quarterround, porterhouse, beef stew and bones for soup broths. She gives us leather belt, leather seats, leather coats and shoes, hats and purses, you name it. The cow is the most prominent giving animal in the world today and has been so through the centuries and millenniums.

Humanity owes a debt to this gentle creature for her selfless service

"How can you expect to govern a country that has two hundred and forty-six kinds of cheese ?"

- Charles de Gaulle (French President and World War II leader)

through the ages. Whether living or dead, cow symbolizes selfless service.

Everything that a cow produces including urine, stool, and every inch of her body, is meant for the good of the world. Any sane man will be appalled by the slaughter of hundreds of thousands of cows every day. To any sane man, it just does not make sense. Such a useful creature is being killed for her flesh. It is like taking an expensive car and demolishing it for its scrap value. We value our machines, but can any machine produce milk from a little grass?

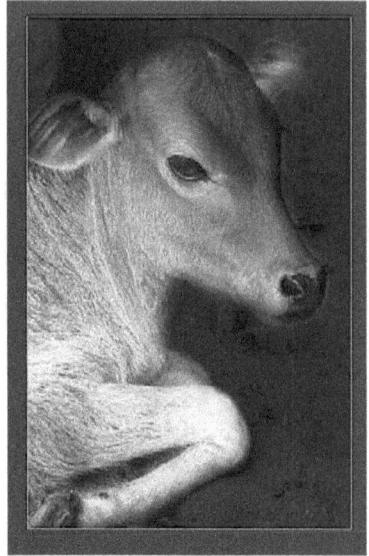

Therefore in Vedic civilization, cow was referred to as 'aghnya'--that which may not be killed under any circumstances. Cow, Bos indicus, is most valuable animal and it is called the 'mother of all'.

Useful When Alive, Useful When Dead

In traditional cultures like India, there is a social class called cobblers. They survive by taking away the dead animals, especially cows. Other animals, they do not care. They are taken by the vultures and others. But when a cow dies, they come and pick it up. A dead cow is as important as an alive one. In India, saying goes for an elephant, "dead or alive, it is worth a hundred thousand rupees." The reason is its ivory bones. Same holds good for the cow. A dead cow offers her flesh, skin, hooves, horns and bones. Every inch of hers is of great utility. Skin is turned into many leather products. Hooves, horns and bones become valuable organic manure.

Before the foreign invasions, cow protection was considered to be a prime governmental duty in India. Kings personally looked after the welfare of the cows. Srimad Bhagavatam speaks of King Prsadhra who would stand all night with a sword to protect cows from wild animals and thieves. Such was his concern for the cows. From these examples we can understand the importance of cow protection. In the very same India today, the government is promoting slaughterhouses for beef consumption and export. How can there be peace and prosperity in the country?

Cow - The Lifeline of Civilizations

Allama Iqbal, a 19th century scholar once remarked, "Ancient civilizations of Greece, Egypt and Rome have all disappeared from this world, but the elements of Indian civilization still continue. Although world-events have been inimical to it for centuries, there is something in Indian civilization which has enabled it to withstand these onslaughts." Similarly Gandhi described European civilization as a 'nine day wonder" while praising Indian civilization to be founded on a solid footing.

It is a fact that many civilizations have come and gone but the vedic civilization continues, at least in traces, even today. India has survived the onslaught of centuries of invasion and colonization. The culture still lives on, even thriving in some pockets.

What is the reason for sustainability of Indian culture? How come the vedic tradition has survived the test of time? One important reason was their ability to live in harmony with the laws of nature and God. And an important part of that balancing act was interweaving every aspect of their existence with cows and bulls.

Living with cows is living on nature's incomes without depleting its capital resources. Modern civilization is utilizing nature's capital resources. These resources like petroleum were accumulated by nature over millions of years, but we have squandered them in just 150 years. How long this reckless lifestyle will go on? In Vedic tradition, cow provided all the necessities of human society. Society reciprocated her services by protecting, serving and adoring her. Bull was regarded as a symbol of religion and also a father because he produced grains by ploughing the fields. Now we have tractors and other agricultural machinery but once the oil runs out, we will have to seek out bulls again (if any left by the time). Of course, over 50% agricultural land in the world is still cultivated with the help of bulls.

Today, in heavily Hindu nations like India and Nepal, cows continue to hold a central place in religious rituals. And in honor of their exalted status, cows roam free. Indeed, it is considered auspicious to give one a snack, a bit of bread, or fruit before breakfast. On the other hand, a citizen can be sent to jail for killing or injuring a cow.

Happy Cows Give More

Cows, Like Us, Want To Be Called By Name!

According to researchers at Newcastle University, happy cows produce more milk, and calling cows by personal names makes them happier.

A study by the university's School of Agriculture, Food and Rural Development, involving 516 farmers across the UK, found that cows that are named and treated with a "more personal touch" can increase milk yields by up to 500 pints a year. The study, published in the journal Anthrozoos, found farmers who named their cows gained a higher yield than those who did not give their cattle names. Dairy farmer Dennis Gibb, who co-owns Eachwick Red House Farm outside Newcastle, said he believed treating every cow as an individual was "vitally important".

Own Personality

Farmer Dennis Gibb says "They aren't just our livelihood, they're part of the family. We love our cows here at Eachwick and every one of them has a name. Collectively we refer to them as 'our ladies' but we know every one of them and each one has her own personality." Dr. Catherine Douglas, who led the research, says: "What our study shows is what many good, caring farmers have long since believed. Our data suggests that, on the whole, UK dairy farmers regard their cows as intelligent beings capable of experiencing a range of emotions. Placing more importance on knowing the individual animals and

As long as man continues to be the ruthless destroyer of lower living beings he will never know health or peace. For as long as men massacre animals, they will kill each other. Indeed, he who sows the seed of murder and pain cannot reap joy and love. - Pythagoras

calling them by name can, at no extra cost to the farmer, also significantly increase milk production."

Cow Dung And Urine - Supremely Valuable Products

In traditional Vedic culture, cow was mainly reared for her manure and urine, not for milk. Milk was only a byproduct. Cow dung and urine were an indispensable part of daily life. Entire agriculture, energy and health requirements depended on these.

These contentions hold good only for the traditional breeds of Asia and Africa and not for the modern breeds of the Western world which

have been selectively bred and modified over the years.

Cow Dung

Traditional Indian life is intimately associated with cow dung which is put to multiple uses. Cow dung is used as a fertilizer, fuel, in tile making, housing, religious rituals, medicine and as a cleaning agent.

Cow dung is accepted as purified and antiseptic. A person can keep stacks of cow dung and it will not create a bad odor. In Calcutta, Dr. Lal Mohan Gosal, a prominent scientist in early 20th century, conducted extensive research on cow dung and proved it to contain all antiseptic properties.

Therefore cow dung, according to Vedic injunctions, practical experience and scientific research, is considered pure. No vedic purificatory ritual is complete without cow dung and cow urine. It is a common practice in rural India even today, to smear cow dung all over the floor and house walls. Practically it makes the atmosphere very refreshing and wards off flies and insects. From time immemorial, Indians have the practice of mopping clay floors with cow dung and sprinkling diluted cow dung at the house entrance. This was to sanitize the entrance and repel harmful microbes. In religious ceremonies, utensils were rinsed with water and cow dung solution. Indians always believed that cow dung has antimicrobial effect and cow urine works as a purifier. Textiles especially the new ones were treated with the ashes of cow dung before they were worn for the first time. In Ayurveda, cow dung dried and burned into ashes is used as a toothpowder and it is considered to be highly antiseptic. Even today, millions are using this toothpowder in India and its popularity is growing.

Some people may find it puzzling because any excreta is foul but Vedas recommend cow dung as a purifier. Vedic authority is considered infallible and perfect. Vedic instructions have been accepted for thousands of years without any research. Accepting vedic authority is like a child accepting food from parents, believing they will never feed him something harmful. The child accepts in good faith, without any reason or analysis. When we visit a restaurant, we accept the supplied food without any laboratory tests. We accept the food in good faith and also because the restaurant is licensed. Without faith, we can not move an inch in life. While boarding a plane, we have to have faith that airline has enough fuel to fly all the way and all equipments have been checked. We board an aircraft and place our lives in the hands of the airline without verifying anything personally.

It's just like with people. There's always an exchange of feelings. Since the cow is a person too, when we become friendly toward them, each cow responds personally. That's how cows are -- the more affectionate you are to them, the more affectionate they are to you. They give more milk and are happier." - Ganendra dasa

62

Of course, faith in Vedic injunctions is not blind but is verifiable by personal experience and observation.

Vedas declare that 'gomaye vasate laksmi', goddess of prosperity resides in cow dung. Indeed at one time when cows outnumbered people, India was the richest nation in the world.

Cow ghee (clarified butter), when poured on burning cow dung cakes, produces copious amounts of oxygen and purifies the air. Studies have proven this and it has been suggested as a tool to fight air pollution.

On 4th May 1985, a news was published in India's national daily, The Hindu, in connection with Bhopal gas tragedy. The news was titled 'Vedic way to beat pollution'.

On the fateful night of December 3, 1984, poisonous MIC gas leaked from Union Carbide plant in Bhopal, India, killing thousands and sickening many more. There were, however two families, Sohan Lal Khushwaha and M.L. Rathore, who lived in the worst affected area but came out unscathed. Later enquiries revealed that both the families were regularly performing yajna or fire sacrifice with cow dung and butter. No casualties were reported from any of the families despite living in the worst hit area.

Therefore cow dung is never considered to be feces but a great purifier. It produces best quality of grains, fruits, and vegetables when used in fields.

Cow Urine

In traditional Indian medicine, cow is considered to be a mobile dispensary and a treasure house of medicines. Cow is regarded as divine source of good health, not only physical but also mental, intellectual and spiritual. Cow urine is an important ingredient in

Knowledge was there. Just like five millions of years ago there was no scientist, analytical laboratory. But the Vedic knowledge is that cow dung is pure. Now you analyze at the present moment scientifically you'll find yes, it is pure. So wherefrom this knowledge came? There is no need of scientist if this knowledge was there. That is Vedic knowledge. ~Srila Prabhupada

panchagavya, five products from cow - milk, curd, butter, urine and dung.

The cow urine is capable of curing several diseases, even ones considered incurable. Atharva veda and other classic texts like Charak samhita, Rajni ghuntu, Amritasagar, Bhavprakash, Sushrut samhita, Ashtanga Sangraha etc. extol glories of cow urine as a panacea and elixir. Ayurveda has elaborate information on its medicinal use classified under Mootravarga. In India gomutra is used by rural population as folklore remedy in almost all the states. Cow urine is said to have qualities of, in technical terms, katu, tikta, kashaya rasa, ushna-veerya (potency) kshra, laghu and deepana prabhava.

Proponents of urine therapy quote sources to indicate that cow urine was not only used in India, but in many parts of the globe. Roman emperors and several European physicians in the 18th Century, as well as the Chinese traditional healers are said to have used not only cow urine but human urine as well.

Today, thousands of patients in India and other places are receiving treatment for diabetes, blood pressure, asthma, psoriasis, eczema, heart attack, blockage in arteries, fits, cancer, AIDS, piles, prostrate, arthritis, migraine, thyroid, ulcer, acidity, constipation, gynecological problems, ear and nose problems, along with many others. Cow urine works like a magic potion.

Cow urine has been found to contains nitrogen, sulphur, phosphate, sodium, manganese, carbolic acid, iron, silicon, chlorine, magnesium, melci, citric, titric, succenic, calcium salts, Vitamin A, B, C, D, E, minerals, lactose, enzymes, creatinine, hormones, gold acids and host of other ingredients which are vital for human health.

Cow urine also contains beneficial volatile salts because these salts destroy acidity; furthermore urine, a natural tonic, eliminates giddiness, tension in nerves, lazy feeling, paralysis, common cold, diseases of brain, nerves, joints and leucorrhea. Cow urine contains copper which works wonders inside our body and removes toxicity.

Cow urine is an excellent pesticide for crops. Also cleaning phenol and mosquito coils are manufactured from it.

Elixir of Life - Cases of Cow Urine Cure

Today, thousands of well-documented cases testify to the miraculous effects of cow urine on human health.

Thousands of cancer patients who lost hope of life and were turned down by modern medicine are leading a healthy and happy life. These cases have been charted for reference by qualified doctors.

There was this patient with highly elevated levels of sugar (400-500), surviving on insulin. After the treatment, there was no necessity to take insulin. In the same way AIDS, asthma, psoriasis, eczema, blood pressure, heart disease, prostrate, piles etc. are also being cured with cow urine.

We can cite many cases of cow urine cure. One Mr. Premchand Rathore was suffering from asthma and isnophilia and used to have severe palpitations and cough. He is perfectly normal now. Mrs. Sharda Jalani was having varicose veins and dysmenorrhea. Whenever she tried to stand up, nerves would swell and cause pain. She was advised surgery for both the problems. But she went for cow urine therapy and is now leading a perfectly normal life. Omprakash Paul suffered a heart attack, he had high levels of cholesterol and chest pain. After taking cow urine therapy he is walking up to four kilometers, chest pain is gone and cholesterol levels are normal. Chandmal Gurjar suffered with cancer of the food pipe four years back, he could not

Krishna is giving very importance, cow-keeping, tending the cows. Personally. Personally taking, protect cows. He is stealing butter, showing us that "These things should be stolen. If you have no money, then you steal and eat." (laughter) You see? These things are eatables. You see. Produce huge quantity of milk, and make so many preparation out of it, and become happy. This is the instruction Krsna is giving. Otherwise what Krsna business, He has got to do some such business? No. He is teaching us. Even the urine in cow is valuable. Stool of cow is valuable. Krsna in His..., while He is crawling on the yard, He captures the tail of a calf and he drags him, and he is smeared with all stools and urine of the cows. Krsna enjoys. He is showing that even the stool and urine of cow is valuable, what to speak of its milk. Cow is so important. -Srila Prabhupada (Lecture, Srimad-Bhagavatam 2.3.19, Los Angeles, June 14, 1972)

take liquids also. Now he is able to eat and drink properly, he is healthy and working in the fields. There are thousands of people who have recovered from serious diseases after resorting to cow urine cure.

Today many AIDS patients are taking cow urine therapy. People who were suffering with migraine and headache for the past 15 years have recovered within six months of the treatment. Whether it is a question of relieving tension or improving the memory power, cow urine seems to be the answer.

One Ms. Sushma Khurana had thyroid complaint. Before treatment her T3 level was 4, T4 was 15, TSH was 0.2. After six months of this treatment, T4 was 9.97, TSH was 1.35 and today she is free from all symptoms. Cow urine has also proven to be a sure cure in cases of eczema, ringworm, itching and other skin problems. Old eczema patients have especially gained from this therapy. Teenage girls can achieve freedom from the menace of pimples and acne.

Panchagavya was traditionally given as the first thing to a woman after she delivers a baby as a recuperative tonic.

For further information on cow urine treatment, Govigyan Anusandhan Kendra in Nagpur, India can be contacted. They are doing pioneering research in this field. Cow urine is available as urine distillate (gomuthra ark), pills (ghanavati) and in various other forms.

Cow Urine Patents

THE U.S. Patent Office (USPTO) grants thousands of patents every week, and yet, the U.S. Patent, 6410059, titled "Pharmaceutical Compositions containing Cow urine Distillate and An Antibiotic" issued to S.P.S. Kanuja and 13 others and assigned to the Council of Scientific And Industrial Research (CSIR), attracted global attention. The Minister For Science And Technology, Government of India, at a Press Conference, said the U.S. Patent made him realize that all traditional practices from Indian systems of medicine have a strong scientific base.

Recently cow urine was granted patent in China for protecting and/or repairing DNA from oxidative damages. The patent no. is 100475221.

Cow urine distillate in a specific amount is scientifically proven to enhance the antimicrobial effects of antibiotic and antifungal agents. US patent no. 6410059 was granted to Indian scientists for the invention on June 25, 2002.

The invention relates to a novel use of cow urine as an activity enhancer and availability facilitator for bioactive molecules, including anti-infective agents. The invention has direct implication in drastically reducing the dosage of antibiotics, drugs and anti-infective agents while increasing the efficiency of absorption of bioactive molecules. This will reduce the cost of treatment and also the side-effects due to toxicity.

Cow Urine In Modern Medicine

Council of Scientific and Industrial Research (CSIR) in India has

Just like when I was walking near the cowshed, heaps of, piles of cow dung was there. So I was explaining to my followers that if such heaps of animal, I mean to say, man stool was heaped up here, nobody would come here. Nobody would come here. But the cow dung, there are so much heaps of cow dung, still, we find it pleasure to go through it. And in the Vedas it is said, "Cow dung is pure." This is called sastra. -Srila Prabhupada (Lecture, Bhagavad-gita 2.22, Hyderabad, November 26, 1972)

developed drugs using cow urine for the treatment of asthma and blood clots. Institute of Microbial Technology (Chandigarh, India) has come out with streptokinase, which is a blood-clot dissolver and plays an important role in heart diseases and brain ailments. The poly-herbal formulation developed by Indian institute of Chemical Biology (Kolkata) that cures asthma contains cow urine. A Pharmaceutical composition by the same institute, comprising an antibiotic and cow urine distillate in certain amount is said to enhance the antimicrobial effect of an antibiotic. Cow urine therapy is set to open doors for treating a wide range of dreaded diseases.

3.

Humanity Owes 'Milk-debt' To Cows

Cow And Bull As Mother And Father

A mother (or mum/mom) is a woman who has raised a child, given birth to a child, and/or supplied the ovum that united with a sperm which grew into a child. Because of the complexity and differences of a mother's social, cultural, and religious definitions and roles, it is challenging to specify a universally acceptable definition for the term.

Vedic definition of 'mother' is quite broad.

atma-mata guroh patni
brahmani raja-patnika
dhenur dhatri tatha prthvi
saptaita matarah smrtah

There are seven mothers. These are, the original mother, the wife of

The fruits? The skin thrown away, and the cow will eat. And in exchange it will give you nice foodstuff, milk. Or it will eat in the grazing ground, some grass. So there is no expenditure of keeping cows, but you get the best food in the world. The proof is that the child born simply can live on milk. That is the proof. So anyone can live only on milk. If you have got the opportunity to drink one pound milk maximum, not very much—half-pound is sufficient; suppose one pound—then you don't require any other foodstuff.
Srila Prabhupada (Lecture, Srimad-Bhagavatam 6.1.21 -- Honolulu, May 21, 1976)

the teacher or spiritual master, the wife of a brahmana, the King's wife, the cow, the nurse and the earth.

Out of these seven mothers, cow occupies a special place. Our own mother nurses us for a while, but cow nurses us for the rest of our life. When we stop taking milk from our mother the cow gladly takes over the role. For this reason the Vedic scriptures refer to her as our mother. This is indicated in the vedic aphorism, 'gavo visvasya matarah.'

As children, nearly all of us were nourished by cow's milk. Certainly one's mother is sacred and should not be killed. It is not a question of India or America. It is a question of common sense and human consideration. If we don't have that, better to learn it from some "primitive worshipers of mythological totems".

Cow's milk is nature's special way to provide nourishment in a civilized way. The barbarians take blood by slitting throats while the civilized take milk. Milk is nothing but a transformation of flesh. It contains all the nutrients of flesh without the need for attendant violence. Milk is a peaceful and nonviolent way of supplementing our nutritional needs.

When I see a cow, it is not an animal to eat; it is a poem of pity for me and I worship it and I shall defend its worship against the whole world.
- Gandhi

We are killing millions of cows in very brutal ways in gigantic slaughterhouses. The United Nations Food and Agriculture Organisation estimated that in 1984 229,249,000 cows and calves were killed for meat production. Since then the beef consumption has more than doubled. This is a very sinful activity. We are suffering in many ways as a result of the enormous karma thus generated.

Where would we be without a generous supply of milk, yogurt, cheese, butter, ice creams, butter milk and ghee. Since time immemorial, everything that gets cooked in the civilized world, has some relationship with these exotic products.

Milk - A Miracle Food and Heavenly Nectar

The Lifeline of Any Civilized Society

Mughal Emperor Akbar once asked his Hindu minister as to which milk was the best. The minister replied that it was buffalo's milk.

Ample food grains can be produced through agricultural enterprises, and profuse supplies of milk, yogurt and ghee can be arranged through cow protection. Abundant honey can be obtained if the forests are protected. Unfortunately, in modern civilization, men are busy killing the cows that are the source of yogurt, milk and ghee, they are cutting down all the trees that supply honey, and they are opening factories to manufacture nuts, bolts, automobiles and wine instead of engaging in agriculture. How can the people be happy? They must suffer from all the misery of materialism. Their bodies become wrinkled and gradually deteriorate until they become almost like dwarves, and a bad odor emanates from their bodies because of unclean perspiration resulting from eating all kinds of nasty things. This is not human civilization. -Srila Prabhupada (Srimad Bhagavatam 5.16.25)

The answer surprised the Emperor, "How foolish! Everyone knows that cow's milk is the best of all." The minister explained, "Sire, You asked about milk and I correctly replied buffalo's. I would have mentioned cow if you would have asked about elixir because cow gives no milk but elixir."

Milk is a complete food. It is so loaded with nutrients that one can survive simply by drinking it. With abundant supply of milk, there is no need for any animal killing and no possibility of diets being deficient in any way.

Up until recently, wandering mendicants in India would stand at the door of the first household they found in the morning. Milk was so plentiful that the householder would immediately offer a pound of milk fresh from the cow. The mendicant would drink it and wander away. That took care of his eating program for the day. A pound of fresh milk is sufficient to supply an adult with all the necessary nutrition. In earlier days, saints and sages practically lived on milk. In India poorest of the men had a few cows, each delivering ten or twenty quarts of milk. No one hesitated to spare a few pounds of milk for the mendicants and other guests.

Srila Sukadeva goswami, the celebrated speaker of Srimad Bhagavatam, followed this simple program of life:

nunam bhagavato brahman
grhesu grha-medhinam
na laksyate hy avasthanam
api go-dohanam kvacit

O powerful brahmana, it is said that you hardly stay in the houses of men long enough to milk a cow. (SB 1.19.39)

Srila Prabhupada explains how generations of highly evolved beings simply survived on milk, "Because in those days in the jungles there were many hermitages. Those who wanted to live secluded life in the jungle, in the forest, they would have their home, very small cottage,

Whoever needs milk, bows to the animal. - *Yiddish Saying*

and their means of living was milk and fruit. They would get fruits from the trees, and the kings would sometimes contribute some cows. So that was sufficient for them. To have some milk from the cow and get the fruits from the trees in the jungle, that was sufficient. That is sufficient still. Anywhere, any part of the world, you can live without any economic problem, provided... There is no question of "provided." Anywhere, you can keep a cow. There is no expenditure. The cow will go out and eat some vegetables and grass, so you haven't got to spend anything for the cow. And when she returns, she gives you milk, nice milk. We are trying to introduce this system in our New Vrindaban scheme. We are keeping there cows, and that place is in Virginia, Moundsville. It is about three miles away from any city or any citizen approach. But they are living very nicely, depending on some vegetables, fruits, and cow's milk. So actually, a man can live very peacefully and healthy life. Not only peacefully. If you are healthy, if your mind is equilibrium, then naturally you are peaceful. So that was a system for the sages and hermits, they used to live on cow's milk and fruits." (Lecture on Srimad Bhagavatam, 2.3.17, Los Angeles, July 12, 1969)

Longer Life for Milk Drinkers - British Researchers

Research undertaken by the Universities of Reading, Cardiff and Bristol of UK this year, has found that drinking milk can lessen the chances of dying from illnesses such as coronary heart disease (CHD) and stroke by up to 15-20%.

In recent times milk has often been portrayed by the media as an unhealthy food. The study, led by Professor Peter Elwood (Cardiff University) together with Professor Ian Givens from the University of Reading's Food Chain and Health Research Theme, aimed to establish whether the health benefits of drinking milk outweigh any dangers that lie in its consumption.

"I have no doubt that it is a part of the destiny of the human race, in its gradual improvement, to leave off eating animals."
- Henry David Thoreau

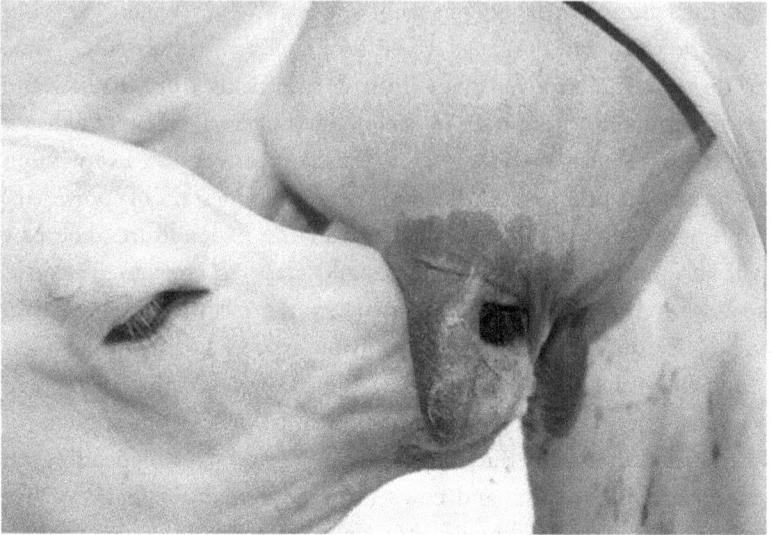

Importantly, this is the first time that disease risk associated with drinking milk has been looked at in relation to the number of deaths which the diseases are responsible for.

The review brought together published evidence from 324 studies of milk consumption as predictors of coronary heart disease (CHD), stroke and diabetes. Data on milk consumption and cancer were based on the recent World Cancer Research Fund report. The outcomes were then compared with current death rates from these diseases.

Professor Givens explains: "While growth and bone health are of great importance to health and function, it is the effects of milk and dairy consumption on chronic disease that are of the greatest relevance to reduced morbidity and survival. Our review made it possible to assess overall whether increased milk consumption provides a survival advantage or not. We believe it does."

Findings clearly showed that when the numbers of deaths from CHD, stroke and colo-rectal cancer were taken into account, there was strong evidence of an overall reduction in the risk of dying from these chronic diseases due to milk consumption. They certainly found no evidence that drinking milk might increase the risk of developing any condition, with the exception of prostate cancer. Put together, there was convincing overall evidence that milk consumption was associated with an increase in survival in Western communities.

The reviewers also believe that increased milk consumption is likely to reduce health care costs substantially due to reduced chronic disease and associated morbidity.

Professor Givens concludes the report thus, "There is an urgent need to understand the mechanisms involved and for focused studies to confirm the epidemiological evidence since this topic has major implications for the agri-food industry."

Srila Prabhupada wrote about impact of milk on human longevity, decades before these findings came out, in his purport to Srimad Bhagavatam (8.6.12), "Milk is compared to nectar, which one can drink to become immortal. Of course, simply drinking milk will not make one immortal, but it can increase the duration of one's life. In modern civilization, men do not think milk to be important, and therefore they do not live very long. Although in this age men can live up to one hundred years, their duration of life is reduced because they do not drink large quantities of milk. This is a sign of Kali-yuga. In Kali-yuga, instead of drinking milk, people prefer to slaughter an animal and eat its flesh. The Supreme Personality of Godhead, in His instructions of Bhagavad-Gita, advises go-raksa, which means cow protection. The cow should be protected, milk should be drawn from the cows, and this milk should be prepared in various ways. One should take ample milk, and thus one can prolong one's life, develop his brain, execute devotional service, and ultimately attain the favor of the Supreme Personality of Godhead. As it is essential to get food grains and water by digging the earth, it is also essential to give protection to the cows and take nectarean milk from their milk bags."

Of course, milk from modern dairy operations is no milk at all. It's loaded with antibiotics, hormones and other chemicals. It's pasteurized, homogenized and what not. It's not given by the cow out of affection for the calf. Its sqeezed out of her after artificially

Cow-slaughter and man-slaughter are in my opinion the two sides of the same coin.
- Gandhi

impregnating her. She never gets to nurse the calf in her short, miserable life. It would be more appropriate to call it her blood rather than milk.

Mother And Father Killing Civilization

Cow is the mother that nourishes us with her milk. Bull is the father who produces grains in the fields. Bull is father also because without his uniting with cow, there is no milk. So modern civilization is a mother and father killing civilization. So how is that we are eating our father and mother? It is a great challenge. Those who are beef-eaters, they are killing their father and mother and becoming implicated in sinful life.

Cow has been a 'life-giver' or 'sustainer of life'. Oxen have pulled the plows on world's farms for centuries. Humanity can never repay the debts of these gentle creatures. Killing them in brutal ways is hardly a way to express our gratitude.

Milk - The Essential Brain Food

As far as eating, sleeping, mating and defence are concerned, there is no difference between human beings and animals. Human beings perform these functions in a more polished way and therefore they can be termed as 'polished animals.' But there is a distinction. Human beings have higher faculties to reflect on philosophy and purpose of life which animals can not. This is where cow milk comes into picture. The body can be maintained by any kind of foods, but cow's milk is particularly essential for developing the finer tissues of the human

For meat-eaters, that is what the Vedic culture recommends: "Eat dogs." As in Korea they are eating dogs, so you also can eat dogs. But don't eat cows until after they have died a natural death. We don't say, "Don't eat." You are so very fond of eating cows. All right, you can eat them, because after their death we have to give them to somebody, some living entity. Generally, cow carcasses are given to the vultures. But then, why only to the vultures? Why not to the modern "civilized" people, who are as good as vultures? [Laughter.] -Srila Prabhupada (Journey of Self Discovery, 6.5: Slaughterhouse Civilization)

brain. This enables one to understand the higher philosophical matters.

Therefore a civilized human being is expected to live on foods comprising fruits, vegetables, grains, sugar and milk. In human society, sufficient milk products should be available. With these products, thousands of wholesome and nourishing preparations can be made. A dull brain cannot comprehend the finer and higher aspects of life. Therefore George Bernard Shaw wrote, 'You are what you eat.' If you eat pigs, you acquire a piggish mentality, if you eat dogs, you acquire doggish traits.

Ungrateful Humanity
Hoping Against Hope For Peace

We kill cows and other animals but they never come to us requesting for food. By nature's arrangement, by God's arrangement, cows and other animals live on grass of which there is profuse supply. They do not eat our foods, rather we make nice preparations from the milk they deliver. Cows convert grass, a worthless thing into milk, a very valuable food. But instead of utilizing her milk, we are utilize her blood. Milk is nothing but transformation of blood and the civilized way to utilize blood is through milk.

By nature's arrangement, by God's will, a cow delivers several pounds of milk but she does not drink an ounce of it although it is her milk! She gives it all to us with only one request, "Take my milk but don't kill me. Let me live, after all I am eating only grass which is of no use to you and delivering in return the most valuable commodity." And the so called civilized beings are inventing sophisticated technologies to kill them in gigantic slaughterhouses and making plans how to kill more and more of them. And they want peace!

Now a days many mothers are unable to breast-feed their newborns

"Civilization is hideously fragile... there's not much between us and the Horrors underneath, just about a coat of varnish." ~C.P. Snow

due to various reasons. And some mothers are able to do so only for a short time due to job and other constraints. It is the cow which takes up this function. All baby feed formulas are based on cow milk. So from the time we are born we take cow's service and later we kill her.

Where is our gratitude? And we think we are civilized. According to vedic injunctions, cow killers fall in the category of naradhamas, lowest of the mankind.

Not Enough Fodder - A Lame Excuse For Killing

When India became independent, the national planning commission proposed that 40% of the cows should be killed because there was not enough fodder to maintain them. Better to kill them rather than let them live a malnourished life. But so many human beings are also malnourished. In fact India has the highest number of malnourished children in the world, even more than Sub-Sahara region. Does it mean they all should be killed? Moreover cow lives on what we discard - chaff, skin, oil cakes, grass and hay - which are of no use to us.

Srila Prabhupada explains, "Krsna has given her the grass to eat. She's not interfering with your food. Why? What right you have got to kill? You have got your own food. The cow has got the grass for her food. You have got food grains. Cow is giving you milk, just to give her protection, that "You take my blood, turn into milk. Please do not kill me." So why these things are happening? Because there is rascal government. Kalina upasrstan. Rascal government. (Lecture, Srimad-Bhagavatam 1.16.22 -- Hawaii, January 18, 1974)

Nutrition Without Meat

Many times the mention of vegetarianism elicits the predictable reaction, "What about protein?"

The ideas that meat has a monopoly on protein and that large amounts of protein are required for energy and strength are both myths.

Of the twenty-two amino acids, all but eight can be synthesized by the body itself, and these eight "essential amino acids" exist in abundance in nonflesh foods. Dairy products, grains, beans and nuts are all concentrated sources of protein. Cheese, peanuts and lentils,

Krishna's laws or nature's law is so nice that a cow is eating grass and producing milk. Now, if you think that grass is the cause of milk, then you are mistaken. It is the laws of Krishna that transforms grass into milk. If you eat..., you eat grass, then you'll die. But the cow, she is eating grass... That also not supplied by your factory. The grass is produced by nature's way. And she is eating that grass and supplying the most nutritious food—milk—and in exchange you are cutting throat. How you can be happy? Such an innocent animal. She is eating grass supplied by God, and instead of grass, if you think that "She is eating grass from the land, American land or my land. She must give me something," she's supplying milk. What reason there is?

So if we human beings, if we forget even ordinary mercy, compassion and gratefulness, then what is that human life?

-Lecture on Srimad Bhagavatam 5.5.1-2 , London , September 13, 1969

for instance, contain more protein per gram than hamburger, pork or steak.

The primary energy source for the body is carbohydrates. Only as a last resort is the body's protein utilized for energy production. Too much protein intake actually reduces the body's energy capacity. In a series of comparative endurance tests conducted by Dr. Irving Flsher of Yale, vegetarians performed twice as well as meat-eaters. Numerous other studies have shown that a proper vegetarian diet provides more nutritional energy than meat. A study by Dr. I. Iotekyo and V. Kilpani at Brussles University showed that vegetarians were able to perform physical tasks two to three times longer than meat-eaters before exhaustion and were recovered from fatigue in one fifth the time needed by the meat-eaters.

By the way, natures biggest and most powerful animals, elephants, rhinoceros etc. are plant eaters. Where do they derive their nutrition from?

A Solution For Compulsive Cow Eaters

Srila Prabhupada presents a solution for those who any how would like to eat meat, "These asuras, they are killing thousands and thousands of cows for getting the skin, only for the skin. So if you are interested in the skin, if you are interested in the flesh, so at least wait for the time the animal will die. There is no doubt about it. So at least let her die natural death. Why you should kill? You can take at that time the skin, the bone, the hoof. Whatever you like, you can

These so-called civilized people -- what is the difference between these rascals and vultures? The vultures also enjoy killing and then eating the dead body. "Make it dead and then enjoy" -- people have become vultures. And their civilization is a vulture civilization. Animal-eaters -- they're like jackals, vultures, dogs. Flesh is not proper food for human beings. Here in the Vedic culture is civilized food, human food: milk, fruit, vegetables, nuts, grains. Let them learn it. Uncivilized rogues, vultures, raksasas [demons] -- and they're leaders.
- Srila Prabhupada (Journey of Self Discovery, 6.5)

take, the flesh. So in India there is a class. They are called chamara. They are called muchi. ... As soon as your animal is dead you give them information. They will come. They'll take the animal. They will get the skin for nothing. So they'll tan it and make shoes for selling. So they will get the raw materials free of charge, so they can make shoes. Tanning with oil and keeping it in the sunshine, the skin becomes soft and durable, and then you can prepare shoes. So there was no problem. And the bones you gather together and keep in a place. In due course of time it will become very good fertilization. And they can eat the flesh also. Only the cobbler class, the muchi class, they eat this cow's flesh after taking the dead animal. So after killing, everyone eats, so why not wait for the natural death and eat it?

But because they are asuras, raksasas, they do not wait for that. They want it fresh. What is that "fresh"? Unless you kill the animal, you cannot eat. So where is freshness? You have to kill her. You have to make it dead, so why not make it naturally dead?" (Lecture, Bhagavad-gita 16.7, Hyderabad, December 15, 1976)

Epitome of Motherly Love

Cow In Witness Stand

On July 6, 1953, a California man named Mike Perkins was formally accused of stealing a calf from a neighbor's ranch, and then branding it with his own ranch's insignia, to conceal the theft. Mike stood before the judge and vehemently denied the charges, saying his neighbor had made the whole thing up out of jealousy.

The judge was going to find Perkins innocent, because the only

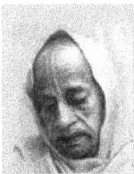

In our New Vrindaban we are maintaining cows and having so many nice preparations, rabri and lagdu and this peda and baraphi and sundesa and rasagulla and yogurt -- varieties enough. The other farmers they come, they are surprised, that "Such nice preparation can be made from milk?" Yes, you do not know. You do not know how to utilize the animal. Ignorance. The milk is also produced out of the blood. (Lecture on Srimad-Bhagavatam 6.1.17, Denver, June 30, 1975)

evidence against him was the others farmer's word. But then he had an idea; he sent the sheriff out to Perkin's ranch, and had him bring to a yard adjacent to the courthouse all of Perkin's calves who were about the age the allegedly stolen calf was reputed to be. Then he sent the sheriff out to the accusing neighbors's ranch, and had him bring to the yard the alleged mother of the stolen calf.

When the mother arrived, she began calling loudly, and seemed to be trying to move towards the roped-in calves. The judge decreed that she be allowed freedom of movement. When she was let go, the mother gave her testimony to the court in no uncertain terms. She went directly over to the calves, nudged her way to one in particular, and began to lick it over and over, right on the hip, where Perkin's brand "P" was located.

There is no need to mention here that Mike Perkins was found guilty.

My friends live across the road from a dairy farm. I will never forget the sounds from the mothers and babies - the heifers and the calfs - when they were separated. I believe this happens when the calves are just days old so the farmers can get all the milk to market. The sound was an utterly overwhelming wall of despair, that's what it was.
It is estimated that for maximum milk production here in Australia, one million calves are taken from their mothers every year, and killed.
-Shannon

Cows Lament A Dead Companion

By Venerable Wuling, March, 2009

My good friend and his wife were visiting their son and daughter-in-law who lived out of town on some acreage that was next to a farm. One morning during the visit, they all awoke to sounds of cows in great distress. Not knowing what was happening, but concerned, the four of them drove over to the farm and found the farmer. When they asked what was happening, he explained.

One of the older cows had died during the night. When he heard the lowing, he went to the field and saw that the cows were all standing around the dead one and lowing in great distress. He quickly got his tractor, dug a deep hole, and maneuvered the dead cow into the hole.

To his amazement the cows positioned themselves around the hole and one or two even tried to climb down into it. The others were around the rim and the older ones pushed their way to the edge of the hole as the younger ones were pushed away to stand behind the older ones. It was as if senior mourners had taken their place before younger ones. The farmer had had the older cows since they were calves and hadn't wanted to kill animals just because they were not productive so the herd had been together for several years.

My friend had shaken his head when he told me of this, saying he had never seen anything like it before.

So do cows cry? Yes, they do, they can feel loss and great sadness and distress. Something we would do well to understand.

A numb mind as they're standing
Is a trait of the bovine ilk.
Naught to do but stand and chew
Munching cud and making their milk.
-Anon

4.

Cow

The Provider Of All Human Necessities

In the natural plan of Vedic living, human society depends on cows for its requirements of economic prosperity, food production, soil fertility, nutrition, healthcare, fuel supply, transport, spiritual well-being, sustainable development, social peace, higher consciousness, development of human qualities, performance of religious duties, environmental protection, ecological preservation, advancement of art & culture, cottage industry etc.

In the universal scheme of creation, fate of species called humans has been attached to that of another, namely cows, to an absolute and overwhelming degree. This implies that welfare and well-being of cows means progress and prosperity and neglect and mistreatment of cows means degradation. Many of the maladies staring in our face today can be traced to this factor – humanity distancing itself from cow protection.

The cow is now forced to tread the path of disgrace and death. The society has reached a stage wherein a dead cow fetches more money than a living one.

Speaking on the troubled condition of our modern world, the late historian Arnold Toynbee once said, "The cause of it [the world's malady] is spiritual. We are suffering from having sold our souls to the pursuit of an objective which is both spiritually wrong and practically unobtainable. We have to reconsider our objective and change it. And until we do this, we shall not have peace, either amongst ourselves or within each of us."

Each one of us is aware of the condition of our urbanized, techno-industrial society that prompted Dr. Tonybee's remarks. Especially in the West, and increasingly in the rest of the world, the mad quest for artificial luxuries has created a chaotic atmosphere. The goal of life? "How much money can I make?" And, "In how many ways can I spend it?" The results of such a philosophy are painfully evident: internationally, we face the risk of war and environmental cataclysm; nationally, crime waves and political corruption rule the land; and individually, we are plagued with anxiety and despair. This is the unfortunate condition of a society without spiritual direction.

Cow & Economic Prosperity

Land and cow are the engines of progress and prosperity. Societies with robust agriculture and cow protection are rich, happy and peaceful. Centuries ago, there were no industries in India. But still it was considered to be the richest nation in the world. There was untold wealth and this brought the invaders and colonizers to her doorstep. Prosperity and affluence was widespread. The reason was India's focus on cow protection and agriculture. As India's focus shifted to industry, especially in the post-independence era, India was reduced to severe poverty. Industries benefitted a few, helping them to become billionaires, but condition of masses considerably deteriorated.

How they will be happy? It is not possible. Most sinful activities. You produce your food. The bull will help you. And the cows will supply you milk. They are considered to be father and mother. Just like father earns money for feeding the children, similarly, the bulls help producing, plowing, producing food grains, and the cow gives milk, mother. And what is this civilization, killing father and mother? This is not good civilization. It will not stay. There will be catastrophe, waiting. Many times it has happened, and it will happen because transgressing the law of nature, or laws of God, is most sinful.
~Srila Prabhupada (Lecture, Bhagavad-gita 13.35, Geneva, June 6, 1974)

People left clean and healthy village life, migrating to cities to live in slums and work is hellish factories. Industrial life offered no security. Any time factories would shut down and workers would have no place to go.

In sanskrit literatures cow is referred to as 'kamadhenu', bestower of all desires. For centuries, land and cows were the standard measure of one's wealth. Currencies and share certificates are only bunch of papers which can come become useless anytime. Even today in many parts of Africa, people keep their investment in cows. A rich family means owning hundreds of cows.

But if you own so many cows, what can you do with all that milk? Srila Prabhupada explains about the utilization of milk:

"Milk is so nice that it cannot be wasted, even a drop. First of all you get milk, that is the Indian system. So there is a big milk pan, and as soon as the milk is drawn it is put into the pan. The pan is in the fire. So as much as you like, drink milk, children, elderly persons. Then at night, when there is no demand for milk, it is converted into yogurt, not wasted. Whatever balance milk is there is converted into yogurt. Then in daytime also you take yogurt, as much as you like. If it is not all consumed, then it is stored in a pot. Then when that pot is enough stored, then you churn it. Churn it, and you get butter and Buttermilk. So again you take buttermilk with chapati and everything, not a single drop is lost. Then the butter, you melt it, convert into ghee and store it, it will stay for years. So not a drop of milk can be wasted. And this butter, because in the village they are eating so much milk products, they do not require butter or ghee. Maybe little, so that is stored. They go to the city. The city men they require, especially. Ghee is very important thing in the city. So they purchase. So in exchange of that money, whatever they want, they purchase in the city and come back. By simply maintaining the cows, their economic problem is solved. Simply maintaining the cows. And to maintain cow there is no difficulty. The boys.... Just like Krishna,

The cow is of the bovine ilk;
One end is moo, the other, milk.
-Ogden Nash

as boy, was taking the cows, the calves, in the fields. They are grazing here and there, and coming back they're giving milk. Only one attendant required to take them into the pasturing ground and bring them back home. You don't require to give them food even. Simply take care, they give milk, and with milk you make so many preparations." *(Garden Conversation, June 10, 1976, Los Angeles)*

When cows graze in fields, they fertilize the soil by their urine and manure. On an average, a cow gives birth to ten calves in her life time and this way also she benefits the keeper.

In the book 'When Histories Collide', the author calculates that the milk from a cow gives 480 lb of digestible dry matter content in a year. In contrast, eating a cow only gives 48 lb of digestible dry matter. Milking cows thus do seem to be around 10 times more productive, in just one year, than eating them. When taken for the full life of a cow, it works out hundreds of times more. This perhaps gives a scientific, secular and common sense explanation for why Hinduism and other religious traditions prohibit eating beef. It is rational for people to avoid eating an animal that, if kept alive, can produce milk and the males can carry loads and pull ploughs.

It has been found that if an average cow's contribution in her lifetime is quantified in money, it comes to millions of rupees. Thus cow represents sound economics. Sustainability of our colossal globalized economy has sharply come under question during recent meltdowns.

Cow & Soil Fertility

World's soil is in danger. Death of soil is death of civilization. Bad soil is bad for global health. All over the world, more than seven and a half million acres of soil has been degraded. That's larger than the U.S. and Canada combined. What remains is ailing as a result of compaction, erosion and salination making it near impossible to plant and adding to greenhouse gases and air pollution. Soil degradation is putting the future of the global population at risk according to a National Geographic article by Charles Mann.

Civil unrest in Latin America, Asia and Africa have been attributed to a lack of food and affordable food as a result of poor soil. *Currently, only 11-percent of the world's land feeds six billion people.* Experts estimate that by 2030 the Earth's population will reach 8.3 billion. Farmers will need to increase food production by 40-percent. But not much soil remains.

Scientists don't know much and don't care either about this critical resource. One solution to this grave problem is switching over to cows instead of chemicals.

Many organic farmers are reviving age old practices of cow dung fertilizers and cow urine pesticides. Popularly known as 'zero-budget farming', it is being practiced on thousands of acres across India. When nourished by mother cow, soil remains fertile for thousands of years but when scorched by chemicals, it dies in 3-4 decades.

Cows eat our leftovers. We take the grains and the rest of the plant is taken by the cows. There is perfect cooperation in the nature's plan. We feed the cow with these leftovers and cow in turn feeds our crops.

In an experiment at the Dairy Research Institute, Ellinbank, Victoria, effects of dairy cow manure on soil fertility was observed. In the soil, extractable soil P (Olsen) was 32mg/kg. After 60 days of

There's something about getting up at 5 a.m., feeding the stock ....and milking a couple of cows before breakfast that gives you a lifelong respect for the price of butter....
-Bill Vaughan

application, extractable soil P increased to 61mg/kg. Extractable soil K (Colwell) almost doubled from 642 mg/kg to 1226 mg/kg in manure treated soils.

Cows return significant quantities of nutrients to pastures through their dung and urine. Up to 65% of the phosphorus (P) eaten in the diet is returned in faeces while approximately 11% and 79% of the consumed potassium (K) is returned in dung and urine respectively (Haynes and Williams, 1993). These nutrients contribute to soil fertility.

In another experiment in Kerala, India, a manure prepared with fermented cow dung and enriched with groundnut cake and neem cake was effective in improving soil quality and enhancing microbial status. In this state famous for black pepper farming, black pepper often suffers from poor growth and wilt disease. This has been linked to the intensive application of chemicals, leading to imbalances in soil micro-flora. This results in the spread of diseases like quick wilt which are caused by soil born pathogens. These problems can be alleviated by improving soil fertility and soil microbial status using fermented cow dung. Application of this manure to black pepper increases growth and improves soil status.

Not withstanding these researches, million of small farms in Asia and Africa still depend on cow dung based fertilizers.

Panchagavya - The Plant Tonic

The ayurvedic literature (Charak Samhita, Sushrut, Gud Nigrah) suggests a number of pharmacological application of the substances obtained from panchagavya. A systematic research is being carried out on chemical nature, biological activity, pharmacology, microbiology and pharmaceutical aspects and mechanism of bioactive compounds in Panchagavya.

Panchagavya has reference in Vrkshayurveda (Vrksha means plants and Ayurveda means health system) also. The texts on Vrkshayurveda are systematizations of the practices the farmers followed at field level, placed in a theoretical framework. It defines certain plant growth stimulants; among them Panchagavya is an important one that enhances the biological efficiency of crop plants and the quality of fruits and vegetables (Natarajan, 2002). The Panchagavya products show excellent agricultural applications. A formulation derived from cow urine and leaves of neem is an excellent pesticide and insect repellent.

Rishi Krishi, a system of Agriculture practiced in India is using Amrit pani (prepared by mixing 20 kg cow dung, 0.125 kg butter, ½ kg honey, ¼ kg ghee) and kept overnight to treat seeds and for spraying on field crops to maintain soil fertility and crop yield (Pathak and Ram, 2002). Individually or system as a whole, biogas slurry with Panchagavya combination is adjudged as the best organic nutritional practice for the sustainability of maize – sunflower – greengram system by its overall performance on growth, productivity and quality of crops, the soil health and economics (Somasundaram, 2003).

Cow & Human Nutrition

The UN estimates that there are approximately 1000 million (1 billion) starving/undernourished people in the world. This is a scandal for humanity when we consider that almost 70% of the grain produce go for meat or fuel production.

Milk is a complete food. In India, even now there are thousands of ascetics who simply live on milk. They are in robust health and do not eat anything else.

Srila Prabhupada explains: "Just like milk is the essence of the blood. The milk is nothing, but it is cow's blood transformed. Just like mother's milk. The mother's milk, wherefrom it comes? It comes from the blood, but transformed in such a way that it becomes nutritious to the child, tasteful to the child. Similarly, cow's milk

As for butter versus margarine, I trust cows more than chemists. -Joan Gussow

also, a most nutritious and valuable food. *(Lecture on Bhagavad-gita 7.3, Montreal, June 3, 1968)*. He further adds, "So from the cows, the milk. And from the milk we can make hundreds of vitaminous foodstuff, hundreds. They're all palatable. So such a nice animal, faithful, peaceful, and beneficial. After taking milk from it, if we kill, does it look very well? Even after the death, the cows supply the skin for your shoes. It is so beneficial. You see. Even after death. While living, he gives you nice milk. You cannot reject milk from the human society. As soon as there is a child born, milk immediately required. Old man, milk is life. Diseased person, milk is life. Invalid, milk is life. So therefore Krishna is teaching by His practical demonstration how He loves this innocent animal, cow. So human society should develop brahminical culture on the basis of protecting cows. *(Lecture, Los Angeles, December 4, 1968)*.

Many doctors blame cow's milk for various diseases. But real culprit is our modern dairy practices. Cows are overloaded with hormones, antibiotics and bio-feeds. They are fed groundup cows. A vegetarian animal is fed cannibalistic diet. Milk is extracted, processed and distributed in most unnatural manner and therefore it leads to ill-health. But when we talk of a happy cow giving milk out of affection for its calf, living in natural surroundings, that milk is as good as or better than our own mother's milk.

Cow's milk, the basis for all other dairy products, promotes strong bones by being a very good source of vitamin D, K and calcium - three nutrients essential to bone health. In addition, cow's milk is a very good source of iodine, a mineral essential for thyroid function; and a very good source of riboflavin and vitamin B12, vitamins that are necessary for cardiovascular health and energy production.

Cow's milk is also a good source of vitamin A, a critical nutrient for immune function, and potassium, a nutrient important for cardiovascular health.

Milk produced by grass fed cows also contains a beneficial fatty acid called conjugated linoleic acid (CLA). Researchers who conducted animal studies with CLA found that this fatty acid inhibits several types of cancer in mice. In-vitro (test tube) studies indicate this compound kills skin, colorectal and breast-cancer cells. Other researches on CLA suggest that this beneficial fat may also help lower cholesterol and prevent atherosclerosis.

Recently "Monocaprin" contained in milk and milk products is reported to possess excellent microbicidal properties and useful against transmitted diseases in humans

According to Ayurveda, the cow ghee (clarified butter) is believed to be the best food for brain functions and general health. It has

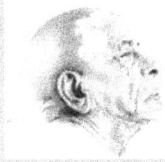

Our first problem is, because we have got this material body, eating. Everyone must eat. So Krsna says in the Bhagavad-gita, annad bhavanti bhutani: [Bg. 3.14] "If there is sufficient food grains, then both man and animal, they become happy." Therefore our first religion is to produce food grain sufficiently to feed everyone. Krsi-go-raksya-vanijyam vaisya-karma svabhava [Bg. 18.44]. This matter has been entrusted to the vaisyas. They should produce sufficient food and give protection to the cows for sufficient milk. Then the whole human society, animal society, will be happy. But we are disobeying the orders or the rules given by God. Instead of producing food, we are producing motorcars. And motor tires, motor parts. And so many other things. And therefore people are starving. The manual labor is being misused. We are disobeying the orders of God. Therefore we are unhappy. I have seen all over the world. There are enough space for producing food grains. And if we actually produce food grain, we can maintain ten times of the present population of the whole world. There is no question of scarcity because God has created everything complete. Purnam idam purnam adaya purnat purnam udacyate [Isopanisad, Invocation]. There cannot be any defect in the creation of God. We have created these defects on account of our disobeying the orders of God. God never said that "motorcar-ad bhavanti bhutani." He never says. But instead of producing food grains, we are producing so many unwanted things. People's energy is engaged for... Just like in America or in every country, so much energy and resources are engaged for preparing war materials. And that means there must be war. And you must be killed; I must be killed. You will kill me; I will kill you. That's all.

(Room Conversation with three Trappist Monks, - March 1, 1975, Atlanta)

many nutritive qualities and is an ideal diet for the heart patients who suffer from cholesterol issues. Cow ghee enhances physical and mental vitality, detoxifies, enhances eyesight, maintains the health of muscles and tendons and keeps the bones stout and flexible.

Curd is another byproduct of milk. In Sanskrit the curd is called 'dadhi'. The ancient Ayurveda specialists like Charaka and Sushruta have described the qualities and usefulness of curd. It is useful in many diseases and it has been described as a tonic. It prevents premature aging, cures diarrhea, dysentery and chronic colitis.

Cow & Energy

Reliance on fossil fuels has largely developed in the last 200 years. Before that, most energy was renewable – animal and human muscle, wood, some wind and water power. The harnessing of new sources of energy, especially coal, about 250 years ago was crucial to the industrial revolution and all the subsequent revolutions.

The world economy is now hooked on to fossil fuels: oil, gas, and coal. This dependency cannot last. All these fuels were formed millions of year ago and once used up cannot be replaced. But before industrial revolution, practically all the energy used was renewable.

For millennia animals have been harnessed to pull carts, carry loads, transport people, haul water, trash harvests, plough, puddle and weed crop fields etc. *Even today, more than half the world's population depends on animal power for much of its energy.* Draught animals operate on more than 50% of the planet's cultivated areas. In the mid 1990s work by draught animals was estimated to be equivalent to a fossil fuel replacement value of US$ 60 billion. Estimates of the number of animals used for power applications range from 300 million upwards.

Oxen are the most frequently used animals and ploughing is the most common function. Almost all species of domestic quadruped are used, however, in a variety of agricultural and transport roles. In agriculture positive effects are seen to be higher crop output, better returns to labour, increased cash income and improved food security.

Despite motorization on all fronts, the use of ox is still often more economic than the use of machinery and vehicles, especially in small scale agriculture and in remote areas. Animals are produced and maintained locally and don't require the infrastructure needed for motorization. Where as the value of machinery depreciates over time, that of animals can appreciate because of growth.

Ox power represents a sustainable and renewable resource of energy. In terms of agriculture, ox power creates a lighter footprint on the earth than a tractor, which tends to compact the soil. Also in terms of the environment, it takes far less resources to produce a team of oxen than a tractor. How many mining operations and how many factories does it require to produce even one tractor? How many drilling and refining operations does it take to fuel it? The "factory" that produces an ox is a cow. For "fuel" the oxen can eat grass and grain which they themselves produce.

And, we should not underestimate the level of benefit that oxen can provide. With the exception of the cultures of the Americas, practically every materially advanced civilization before the crusades – including China, India, the Middle East, North Africa and Europe – relied on oxen for agriculture, transport, grinding grains and even building. Many of the great projects of ancient times were all accomplished without the incredible level of pollution it would take to recreate such structures today.

Srila Prabhupada advises, "Petrol is required for long-distance transport, but if you are localized, there is no question of such

Man through the cow is enjoined to realize his identity with all that lives. – Gandhi

transport. You don't require petrol.... The oxen will solve the problem of transport."

The tractor is a real sore point in agriculture. Tractors are expensive to operate. This expense partly explains why hundreds of thousands of small farms collapse every year. But ox power, though slower, is far more efficient.

Also, oxen provide free fertilizer, preserve precious topsoil, and don't foul the atmosphere with carbon monoxide. Bovine waste, when mixed in the traditional way with straw, is the world's best fertilizer. And when the animal dies, its skin can be processed into leather.

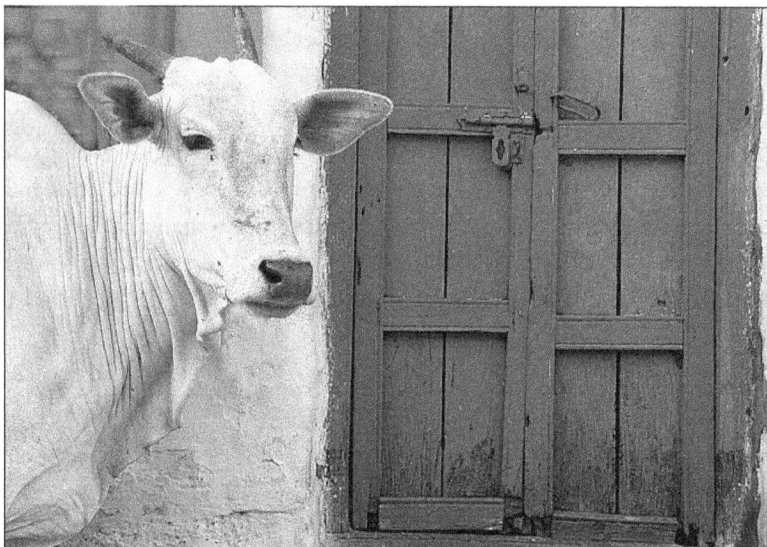

Turning to Gandhi for inspiration, we find that a key requirement for building peace is to provide full employment by emphasizing localized production for localized markets. Gandhi stressed that everything which can be produced locally should be, even if the local economy is less efficient at its production. Since time immemorial, human cultures have lived with and protected cows. Cows have provided many essential services to humanity for very little maintenance. They are an inseparable part of God's efficient system for human civilization.

Dr. Vandana Shiva, an ecologist, comments on India's recent cattle policy while calling it a policy of ecocide of indigenous cattle breeds and a policy of genocide for India's small farmers: "The traditional approach to livestock is based on diversity, decentralisation, sustainability and equity. Our cattle are not just milk machines or meat machines. They are sentient beings who serve human communities through their multidimensional role in agriculture."

"On the other hand," continues Shiva, " externally driven projects, programs and policies emerging from industrial societies treat cattle as one-dimensional machines which are maintained with capital intensive and environmentally intensive inputs and which provide a single output - either milk or meat. Polices based on this approach are characterised by monocultures, concentration and centralisation, non-sustainability and inequality."

Thus whether we like it or not, when fossil fuels bid us good bye, we will have to revert back to bull power for fulfilling our energy requirements.

Cow & Healthcare

Indian science of medicine, known as Ayurveda, describes thousands of medicines based on cow products like milk, curd, ghee, cow urine and cow dung. Called 'Pancha-gavya', these traditional medicines are gaining popularity and many incurable diseases are being cured from with these medicines. Ayurvedic concept of health is called 'holistic' which means not only physical but also mental and spiritual well-being.

Global Health Care Alternative

Considering the fact that more than 70% of the global population do not have access to modern health care, panchagavya can play an important role in improving global health. Health care today means paying pharmaceutical giants who are making obscene profits out of people's miseries. How many can afford such treatment? Panchagavya presents, on a grass root level, a very practical alternative to corporate health care. Last year, out of $600 billion spent on health care worldwide, more than half was spent in the US alone, which is just the 4% of world's population. If 4% of the population uses up more than 50% of the world's health budget, then what will happen to the rest 96% population.

Cow Urine

Cow urine is antifungal, antibacterial, antibiotic, antiallergic, and antimicrobial. There is a great demand for it in India, especially among cancer patients. Milk is around Rs. 15-20 a litre where as cow urine is selling Rs 30-40 a litre. From constipation to cancer, diarrhea to diabetes, advocates of cow urine are offering to cure nearly everything.

Ayurveda says that illness is caused by an imbalance of three elements air (vata), bile (pitta) and mucous (kapha) in the body. Cow urine balances these three elements, 'Samya dosharogata' meaning when three elements are in balance, there are no diseases.

A herbal preparation popular in Nigeria is based on cow's urine and some herbs. It is called Cow urine concoction (CUC). Over fifty chemical compounds have been identified in CUC. Its major pharmacological actions include anticonvulsant and hypoglycemic effects.

Cow urine works wonders in recuperating dead cells, especially the cancerous ones. So it is being used in the treatment of cancer with considerable success.

Also women apply cow urine in their hairs to get rid of lice.

For The Critics of Cow Urine

If urine of a mare can be used, why not the cow's. Premarin is the commercial name for a compound drug which is isolated from mare's urine. It is manufactured by Wyeth Pharmaceuticals and has been marketed since 1942. Premarin is a form of hormone replacement therapy. Since ages, Arabs have used camel urine to treat ailments.

Saying goes that one living being's food is poison for another. What cow rejects can be perfectly useful for humans. Body excretes harmful waste materials. But these waste materials can be used by other species.

Why do we accept oxygen that is excreted by plants and why do plants take our excreta as manure? It is a natural law that living beings depend upon one another. Hogs relish human excreta more than anything else.

What to speak of cow urine, in many megacities, sewage is being recycled to supply drinking water. This is called toilet to tap water system.

Cow & Housing

In mud houses in India, cow dung is used to line flooring and walls because of its insect repellent properties. It stops insects and pests from burrowing in the walls. In cold places cow dung is used to line the walls for its thermal insulation property. Cow dung is also used in tropical areas as an mosquito repellent. Many companies are manufacturing cow dung based mosquito coils. It was used extensively in Indian railways to seal smoke boxes on steam locomotives.

Cow & Fuel Supply

Cow dung is an excellent fuel. It helps to preserve world's fossil fuel reserves. It is odorless and burns without scorching, giving a slow, even heat. A housewife can count on leaving her pots unattended all day or return any time to a preheated griddle for a short-order cooking. To replace dung with coal would cost India $15 billion per year, not counting the environmental costs.

Cow dung is used extensively to produce cooking gas called gobar gas. India is a leader in gobar gas technology, and there are hundreds of thousands of gobar gas plants in India. A gobar gas plant is designed in the following way.

A sealed water-tight circular pit, normally about ten feet deep, is made of concrete to which cow manure is added regularly. Alternate materials may be used for constructing this pit as desired. A wall is built across the middle of the pit, extending from the bottom almost to the top.

The manure is mixed with water in the intake basin which flows through the piping to the bottom of the left side. This side of the cylinder gradually fills and overflows to the right side. When both sides of the cylinder are full, the manure effluent flows out from the bottom of the right side each time more raw manure is added to the left.

Manure residue from the decomposition process comes out in a concentrated form and is used as a fertilizer. What comes out on the right is of more value as a fertilizer than the raw manure. So the methane gas produced from this decomposition is an added byproduct which is literally "something for nothing," after the initial construction expense.

The concoction produces methane which rises to the top and collects under a large metal dome. As the gas builds pressure it is routed via a rubber tube to a gas stove in a kitchen where it is used for cooking. This gas can be used for generating power, lighting up the house or running vehicles also.

Cow & Transport

The world cattle population is close to one billion out of which over 200 million indigenous cows reside in India. This accounts for one-fifth of the world's cattle population. In more recent years, some economists have come to agree that cow is essential to world's economy. Cows are the greatest natural resource. They eat only grass --which grows everywhere--and generates more power than all of the generating plants in developing countries. They also produce fuel, fertilizer, and nutrition in abundance. Many developing countries run on bullock power. *In India, some 15 million bullock carts move approximately 15 billion tons of goods across the nation.* Newer studies in energetics have shown that bullocks do two-thirds of the work on the average farm in developing countries. Electricity and fossil fuels account for only 10%. Bullocks not only pull heavy loads, but also grind the sugarcane and turn the linseed oil presses. In India itself, converting from bullocks to machinery would cost an estimated $30 billion plus maintenance and replacement costs.

Agricultural is still the mainstay of developing economies like India. Cow breeding and cow preservation are integral to it. 75 per cent of Indians live in villages and derive the greatest benefits from cows and bullocks. Despite the compulsions of modernism, tractors are not suitable for Indian land holdings unlike in the US and UK. In US the land available to each person is around 14 acre; in India it is around 0.70 acre. A tractor consumes diesel, creates pollution, doesn't eat grass nor produces dung for manure. So for Indian conditions ploughing is still ideal. Even Albert Einstein, in a letter to Sir CV Raman, wrote: "Tell the people of India, that if they want to survive and show the world path to survive, then they should forget about tractor and preserve their ancient tradition of ploughing."

Cow & Sustainable Development

Growth and progress of the modern world is like progress of the moths into fire. We are running at great speed but we are on the wrong road. We are too busy with the speedometer to see the milestone. Vedic India presents an ideal example of sustainable development wherein perfect harmony exists between man and nature. Srimad Bhagavatam presents a picture of cow based sustainable development five thousand years ago during the rule of Pandava dynasty.

Srila Prabhupada says, "So Maharaja Yudhisthira was so pious that during his reign time, kamam vavarsa parjanyah [SB 1.10.4]. There was regular rainfall and everything was produced nicely. Sarva-kama-dugha mahi. Sarva-kama. The, another side is that you don't require industries, trade. You don't require. If you have got land and cow, then everything is complete. This is basic principle of Vedic civilization. Have some land. Have some cows. Dhanyena dhanavan gavayah dhanavan. Not industry. There is no need of industry. Because you want some food, nice food, nice milk, nice fruit, that will be produced by nature. You cannot manufacture all these things in the factory. So therefore at the present moment, the big, big factories, they are the activities of the asuras, ugra-karma. All the people are dragged in the city, industrial area, to engage them in the produce of iron bars, big, big iron bars, Tata iron industry, and so many other industries.

Capitalists, they have drawn all the innocent people from the village. And they think that "We are getting fat salary." But what is the use of fat salary? One side you get fat salary; another side you have to purchase three rupees a kilo rice. Finish your salary. This is going on. Let them produce their own food. Let them have some land. Let there be cows. Let cows become happy.

Now here is very important word, that payasodhasvatir muda, udhasvatir muda. The cows were very jolly because they can understand whether they are going to be killed or not. Because they have got, they're animal, they have got sense. I have seen in your country, almost all cows are crying. Because in the beginning, all the calves are taken away and slaughtered in their presence. Perhaps you know. So what is the position of the cow? I have seen when we purchased some cows, the calves had already been taken away. The cow was crying, regular tears were gliding down. So they can understand that... Who cannot understand? Suppose if you are taken to the concentrated camp? Just like the Germans did. What is the meaning of concentrated...? That you'll be killed after some days. So how can you be happy? If you are already informed, condemned to death, and kept in a concentration camp, will you be happy? Similarly, when these people take these cows to the slaughterhouse, animal stock room, they can understand. Very recently, about few years ago, some..., that animal stock store was some way or other broken and all the cows began to run... Perhaps you know. It was published in the... And they were shot down. Shot to death. They were fleeing like anything, that "We shall save ourselves."

So if the cows are not happy, if they are always afraid, that "This rascal will kill us at any moment," then how they can be happy? There was no such thing. Therefore it is said: muda. Muda. Happy. And as soon as the cows are happy, you not only get sufficient milk, but the pasturing ground, I mean to say, ground, becomes moist with milk. So much milk supplied. Here it is stated, payasa udhasvatir muda. Yes. There is another description. Formerly, Krsna's cows, when they were passing on, the whole road will be moistened with milk. Milk supply was so sufficient. Simply manufacture butter, milk products, dahi... Distribute. Krsna was distributing amongst the monkeys even: "Take," the monkey, "come on."

So by Krsna's grace if we actually become dharmic, follow Krsna, the milk supply will be so profuse that everyone, even the animals can take the butter and yogurt. That is wanted. That is civilization. Produce sufficient quantity of grains, let the milk, cows, supply sufficient quantity of milk. All economic question solved. There is no use of industry. No use of man's going fifty miles to work. No, there is no need. Simply land and cows. Here is the statement. Kamam parjanyah, vavarsa parjanyah sarva-kama-dugha. Everything you'll get from the land. Even luxury articles. What can be more luxurious article than the jewels? The jewels are also produced. The medicine is produced, the minerals are produced, gold is produced, diamond is produced from the earth. Sarva-kama-dugha. You get everything. Make your civilization very perfect, very luxurious simply by satisfying Krsna. This is Krsna consciousness movement." *(Lecture, Srimad-Bhagavatam 1.10.4 -- Mayapura, June 19, 1973)*

5.

Cow - A Symbol Of Innocence, Purity And Magnanimity
A Gentle And Tender Creature

Cows are guileless in their behaviour and peaceful in their demeanour. Any other species including humans fight when flocked together but cows never fight. Cows and bulls sitting peacefully in pastures and chewing cud reflect a peaceful and happy society. No wonder, the magnanimous cow acts as a surrogate mother by providing milk to human beings for the whole life.

Vedic culture requires us to take bath every time we touch any excrement, including our own. But cow dung is used right in the sanctum sanctorum of temples and indeed in worshiping deities, cow's urine and stool are essential ingredients.

That is the reason cow has been assigned such an elevated status in vedic culture.

In this material world, there are three modes of nature known as goodness, passion and ignorance. Everything and every being exists in one of these three modes. Goodness is first class, passion is second and ignorance is third class. Living beings in mode of goodness are

Cows are amongst the gentlest of breathing creatures; none show more passionate tenderness to their young when deprived of them; and, in short, I am not ashamed to profess a deep love for these quiet creatures. - Thomas de Quincey

considered pious and living beings in mode of ignorance are considered impious.

For example, there are trees which are third class, good for only fuel. Then there are trees which are first class, giving nice fruits and flowers. Then there are pious birds like ducks, swans, peacocks and impious birds like crows and vultures. Amongst animals also, dogs, jackals, hyenas are considered impious and animals like cows and deers are considered pious. Cow is in fact the most pious of all the creatures.

Cow Who Taught What It Means To Care

An Excerpt from 'Critical Problems and their Compassionate Solutions' by Ajahn Brahm

"I arrived early to my meditation class in a low-security prison. A criminal whom I had never seen before was waiting to speak with me. He was a giant of a man with bushy hair, beard and tattooed arms.

So from the cows, the milk. And from the milk we can make hundreds of vitaminous foodstuff, hundreds. They're all palatable. So such a nice animal, faithful, peaceful, and beneficial. After taking milk from it, if we kill, does it look very well? Even after the death, the cows supply the skin for your shoes. It is so beneficial. You see. Even after death. While living, he gives you nice milk. You cannot reject milk from the human society. As soon as there is a child born, milk immediately required. Old man, milk is life. Diseased person, milk is life. Invalid, milk is life. So therefore Krsna is teaching by His practical demonstration how He loves this innocent animal, cow.
- Srila Prabhupada (Lecture , Los Angeles, December 4, 1968)

The scars on his face told me she had been in many a violent fight. He looked so fearsome that I wondered why he was coming to learn meditation. He wasn't the type. I was wrong of course. He told me that something had happened a few days before that spooked the hell out of him.

As he started speaking, I picked up his thick Ulster accent. To give me some background, he told me that he had grown up in the violent streets of Belfast. His first stabbing was when he was seven years old. The school bully had demanded the money he had for his lunch. He said no. The bully took out a long knife and asked for the money a second time. He thought the bully was bluffing and refused to give it again. The bully never asked a third time, he just plunged the knife into the seven year old boy's arm, drew it out and walked away. He told me that he ran to his father's nearby house in shock with blood streaming down his arm. His unemployed father took one look at the wound and led his son into the kitchen, but not to dress the wound. The father opened a drawer, took out a big kitchen knife, gave it to his son, and ordered him to go back to school and stab the bully back. That was how he had been brought up. If he hadn't grown up to be so big and strong, he would have long been dead.

The jail was a prison farm where short-term prisoners, and long-term prisoners close to release, could be prepared for life outside by learning a trade in the farming industry. Furthermore, the produce from the prison farm would supply all the prisons around Perth with inexpensive food, thus keeping down costs.

Australian farms grow cows, sheep and pigs, not just wheat and vegetables; so did the prison farm. But unlike other farms, the prison farm had its own on-site slaughterhouse. Every prisoner had to have a job on the prison farm. I was informed by many of the inmates that the most sought-after jobs were in the slaughterhouse. These jobs

The bull and the cow are the symbols of the most offenseless living beings because even the stool and urine of these animals are utilized to benefit human society.
-Srila Prabhupada (Srimad Bhagavatam 1.17.13)

were especially popular with violent offenders. And the most sought-after job of all, which one had to fight for, was the job of the slaughterer himself. That giant and fearsome Irishman was the slaughterer.

He described the slaughterhouse to me; super-strong stainless steel railings, wide at the opening but narrowing down to a single channel inside the building, just wide enough for one animal to pass through at a time. Next to the narrow channel, raised on a platform, he would stand with the electric gun. Cows, sheep and pigs would be forced into the stainless steel funnel using dogs and cattle prods. He said they would always scream, each in their own way, and try to escape. They could smell death, hear death and feel death. When an animal was alongside his platform it would be writhing, wriggling and moaning in full voice. Even though his gun could kill a large bull with a single high-voltage charge, the animal would never stand still long enough for him to aim properly. So it was one shot to stun, next shot to kill. One shot to stun, next shot to kill. Animal after animal. Day after day.

The Irishman started to become excited as he moved to the occurrence, only a few days before, that had unsettled him so much. He started to swear. In what followed he kept repeating, 'This is the God f___ing truth!' as if afraid I would not believe him.

That day they needed beef for the prisons around Perth so they

The cow to me is a sermon on pity.
- Gandhi

were slaughtering cows. One shot to stun, next shot to kill. He was well into a normal day of killing when a cow came up he had never seen before. This cow was silent. There wasn't even a whimper. Its head was down as it walked purposely, voluntarily, slowly into position next to the platform. It did not writhe, wriggle or try to escape. Once in position the cow lifted her head and stared at her executioner, absolutely still.

The Irishman hadn't seen anything even close to this before. His mind went numb with confusion. He couldn't lift his gun; nor could he take his eyes away from the eyes of the cow. The cow was looking right inside him. He slipped into timeless spaces. He couldn't tell me how long it took, but as the cow held him in eye contact, he noticed something that shook him even more. Cows have very big eyes. He saw in the left eye of the cow, above the lower eye lid, water began to gather. The water grew and grew until it was too much for the eyelid to hold. It began to trickle slowly all the way down her cheek forming a glistening line of tears.

Long closed doors were opening slowly to his heart. As he looked in disbelief, he saw in the right eye of the cow, above the lower eyelid, more water gathering, growing by the moment, until it too was more than the eyelid could contain. A second stream of water trickled down her face. And the man broke down. The cow was crying.

He told me that he threw down his gun, swore to the fullest extent of his considerable capacity to the prison officers that they could do whatever they liked to him, but "THAT COW AIN'T DYING!"

He ended by telling me that he was vegetarian now. That story was true. Other inmates of the prison farm confirmed it for me. The cow that cried taught one of the most violent of men what it means to care."

Cows Need Tender Loving Care

Dairy industry is increasingly becoming profit oriented and cows are increasingly being treated as milk or meat machines. There is growing desensitization to animal suffering.

Globally, year 2007 saw a higher percentage of dairy cows dying due to neglect than any other previous times. The Dairy 2007 USDA survey reported that 5.7 percent of cows died on-farm across the US in 2006. That's an increase from 4.8 percent in the 2002 survey and 3.8 percent in the 1996 survey. Besides being an economic issue (replacing dead cows costs money), this also indicates an animal welfare problem.

More dairy cows are dying, but treating them as individuals instead of groups could help because each cow has an individual personality.

The same survey indicates that the single largest cause of cow death as reported by producers was lameness or injury (20 percent), followed by mastitis (16.5 percent), calving problems (15.2 percent), and unknown reasons (15 percent).

These surveys emphasize treating cow as a sentient being with unique personality traits. If treated well, cows can deliver a lot. There are many dairy operations where loving care has made all the difference.

At ISKCON center in Mayapur India, they treat cows kindly. It's true for many places in India but the Krishna devotees have created an old age home for cows that really does it right. In West Bengal, as else where in India now, older dry cows are neglected and let off in streets or sold off to butchers. The Krishna center in Mayapur invites the farmers to donate their dry cows to them. On arrival, the devotees give each cow a name, her own stall (with name painted overhead) and play melodious prayer songs through overhead speakers all day long. Guess what happens? The cows start giving milk again. So much

Krsna's laws or nature's law is so nice that a cow is eating grass and producing milk. Now, if you think that grass is the cause of milk, then you are mistaken. It is the laws of Krsna that transforms grass into milk. If you eat..., you eat grass, then you'll die. But the cow, she is eating grass... That also not supplied by your factory. The grass is produced by nature's way. And she is eating that grass and supplying the most nutritious food -- milk -- and in exchange you are cutting throat. How you can be happy? Such an innocent animal.

-Srila Prabhupada (Lecture, Srimad-Bhagavatam 5.5.1-2, London September 13, 1969)

milk that it provides for all the yoghurt, butter and milk needs of the entire community, with surplus to sell.

In another instance, Baba Sri Bhadariya Maharaj is doing a commendable work in the desert area of Pokhran, India. His ashram provides shelter to nearly 20,000 stray cows. Sick, old and injured

cows are brought from far off places but loving and tender care turns them into healthy, milching cows again. Baba is providing free milk and butter milk to the travelers in the desert.

After all, milk is produced out of affection and giving milk is a motherly function performed out of love for the offspring.

6.

To Further The Cause of Cow Protection

Some Practical Steps

The first step in cow protection would be to stop eating them. Of course, in many cultures like Hindus of India, abstaining from beef is already in practice.

Every household can adopt a cow or can feel responsible for the livelihood of a cow. It does not necessarily mean personally taking care but it could be sponsoring a cow in one of the organizations that look after cows.

Traditional Hindus had many interesting practices related to cow protection which one may adapt as far as possible. Many families still continue their tradition in this regard.

In many homes, the first chapati (Indian bread) they cook is kept aside for cows. Since cooking is done at least twice a day, cows get a minimum of two chapatis from each family. The offering to God or saying grace is done with the second chapati. This means the cow's share precedes that of God's. Also vegetable and fruit peels and other leftovers are carefully collected for feeding them. Jaggery and molasses are their favorites and many families keep sufficient stock of these.

On social occasions like childbirth, marriage or bereavement, a portion of expenditure is dedicated towards cow protection. But these days billions of rupees are spent in lavish Hindu ceremonies like marriages but not a penny is spared for this cause. It was a tradition to seek the blessings of cow and bull on these auspicious occasions. When some one in the family fell sick, a cow would be fed and a prayer would be offered for quick recovery. Also water was kept in front of the house for stray cows and other animals and birds.

It was believed that a family would be comfortable if it kept its cows comfortably. A society's well-being was gauged by the well-being of the cows. Vedic literatures mention that an entire family or nation can be doomed if the cows are in distress. If this is true than today's society is unhappy because it has failed in its duty of cow protection.

Also it was common to set aside a certain percentage of income for the cows. Many families even now set aside one rupee a day for this purpose. When famine strikes, some families go out of their way to take care of the cows. It is not uncommon to find skinny human beings and well-fed cows. Traditionally, old cows and bulls were looked after just like old parents, with entire family tending to their needs.

Traditional educational system, taught in the gurukulas, emphasized the importance of cow protection. Today's educational system discusses the benefits of cow slaughter and beef export. India is already a world leader in beef export. Many Brazilian and Australian companies are unable to compete and going bankrupt.

The virtue of kindness has to be inculcated from a tender age. Cow protection needs to be included in the standard curriculum. If Garuda (bird carrier of Lord Vishnu) can be the national symbol of an Islamic country like Indonesia, cow can definitely be the national animal of India.

In India, cow protection remains a hotly debated issue. Many organizations are struggling to get cow slaughter completely banned while the government is trying to modernize slaughterhouses and augment beef export earnings.

If cow keeping becomes economically viable, that will immediately stop cow slaughter in India. Farmers often sell their cattle unwillingly out of economic pressure. If people start using cow products like toothpaste, soaps, medicines, fertilizers, pesticides etc., there will be no more cows available for slaughter.

Main utility of cow is her dung and urine. Milk was always considered a byproduct. Today cow's main function is to provide milk and meat.

Leaving aside all cow products, if Indians just take two spoons of cow urine distillate every morning, it will save many cows and health of the nation will improve dramatically. In turn it will save billions in health care. Cow based rural economy is the only way to go for the third world countries like India. That's the only way the village economies can flourish and the masses can rise above the poverty line.

Cow is a mobile dispensary. Over 150 medicines are being manufactured out of cow products now. These medicines, known as 'panchagavya chikitsa' work like a charm.

This is the only viable system of medicine for Indian masses. Modern health care is a failure even in a country like America where it remains a hotly debated issue. Health care is a multi-trillion dollar industry with strong muscle and lobbying power. India in next five years is investing $216 billion in health care infrastructure but it will remain out of reach for over 90% of the population. Health care system based on cow products is cheap and effective. It is highly suitable for rural masses who have easy access to cows. Panchagavya centers can be established on village level not only in India but all over the third world.

Now many medical colleges have started courses on panchagavya and dedicated cow science universities (called Kamdhenu visvavidyalaya) are coming up.

Cow is the single fact which can unite numerous factions of Hinduism. No matter what is one's path, every Hindu agrees on the universal practice of cow protection. In Hinduism, different schools of philosophical thought exist and some of them don't see each other eye to eye. But still there is complete agreement on one point - cow protection.

Today's younger generation is blamed for not showing enough respect to elders. In traditional India, children were taught to respect mother cow and bull from an early age and this training extended to

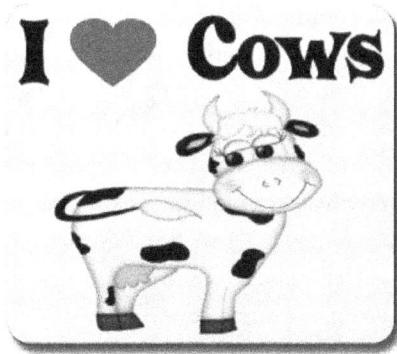

their original parents. As old cows and bulls are slaughtered now, a time will come when old parents would similarly be killed and their organs exported.

Every town and village in India had cow service cooperatives known as pinjarapoles. Retired cows passed their last days there in comfort and dignity. The local communities organized and executed this on a cooperative basis.

No cow should be left to loiter on Indian streets. They lead a very miserable life. Suffering from hunger, thirst and disease, they are often injured by moving vehicles. How can any sane person turn a blind eye to such a pathetic sight. Every town and city should have veterinary hospital for sick and injured cows. *CareforCows.org* is doing a commendable work in this connection in Vraja area of north India. In Delhi and NCR area, *Love4cow Trust* is spearheading the efforts in caring for stray cows. They have a truck with hydraulic system to carry sick or injured cows. Similar facilities are required for every Indian town and city.

Biogas and fertilizer from cow dung represent humanity's future when the fossil fuels run out. A large family can meet all its requirement of energy and fertilizer from just two cows. Every home can be self-sufficient and grow energy in its own backyard.

Production techniques of various cow products should be made available on village level to make it a widespread cottage industry. Government can subsidize the machinery and investment just as it subsidizes slaughterhouses and beef production.

A nationwide awareness and consciousness has to be created. Citizens should vote for a political party which has cow protection in its agenda. All kingdoms in India set aside a portion of state outlay towards cow protection. Today's government is dedicating its resources for killing more and more cows.

Murder is one thing but a murder involving exceptional brutality or cruelty is a different thing altogether. For days and weeks on end, cows are piled on top of one another and shipped to far distant places. Most of them are injured and many die. Its long cruel road to the slaughterhouse. This is their final journey after a lifetime of service.

This is the reward these innocent creatures receive after giving so much to the human race. These are the last frontiers of inhumanity. A public awareness has to be created against this barbarism and culprits should be brought to book. Cruel transport is illegal but the police is always hand in gloves with the butchers.

Cow is also a mobile temple. She is said to house the Supreme Lord and all the functional deities of material world. Cows and bulls are represented in all Hindu temples and home altars.

There is need for more seminars and workshops on the subject, both on local and international level.

If we examine the world history in last two thousand years, we find that all the revolutions were inspired by literature. There is need for more printed material on the subject to reach every home. Also there is need for more material for world wide web.

THE AUTHOR

Dr. Sahadeva dasa (Sanjay Shah), born in December 1966, is a monk in vaisnava tradition. Coming from a prominent family of Rajasthan, he graduated in commerce from St.Xaviers College, Kolkata and then went on to complete his CA (Chartered Accountancy) and ICWA (Cost and works Accountancy) with national ranks. Later he received his doctorate.

For close to last two decades, he is leading a monk's life and he has made serving God and humanity as his life's mission. His areas of work include research in Vedic and contemporary thought, Corporate and educational training, social work and counselling, travelling in India and aborad, writing books and of course, practicing spiritual life and spreading awareness about the same.

He is also an accomplished musician, composer, singer, instruments player and sound engineer. He has more than a dozen albums to his credit so far. His varied interests include alternative holistic living, vedic studies, social criticism, environment, linguistics, history, art & crafts, nature studies, web technologies etc.

His earlier books, Oil - A Global Crisis and Its Solutions (oilCrisisSolutions.com), End of Modern Civilization and Alternative future (EndofCivilization.net) have been acclaimed internationally. More information is available on his portal - DrDasa.com.

OTHER BOOKS BY THE AUTHOR

Oil - Final Countdown To A Global Crisis And Its Solutions

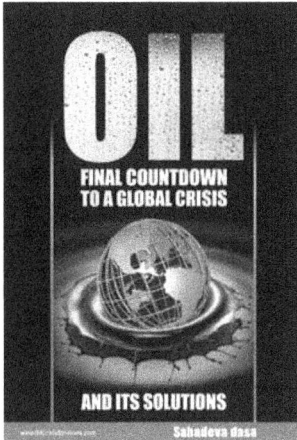

This book examines the lifeline of modern living - petroleum. In our veins today, what flows is petroleum. Every aspect of our life, from food to transport to housing, it is all petroleum based. Either it's petroleum or it's nothing. Our existence is draped in layers of petroleum. This book is a bible on the subject and covers every conceivable aspect of it, from its strategic importance to future prospects. Then the book goes on to delineate important strategic solutions to an unprecedented crisis that's coming our way. Pages-330   www.OilCrisisSolutions.com

ISBN 978-81-909760-0-8

End of Modern Civilization And Alternative Future

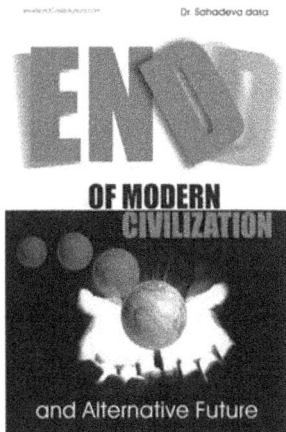

This book is an authoritative work in civilizational studies as it relates to our future. Dr. Dasa studied the human civilizations of last 5000 years and the reasons these civilizations collapsed. Each of them collapsed due to one or two factors like neglect of soil, moral degradation or leadership crisis but in our present day civilization, all these factors along with many more are operational. Then the book goes on to chalk out the alternative future for mankind.

Pages-440   www.EndofCivilization.net

ISBN 978-81-909760-1-5

Cow And Humanity - Made For Each Other

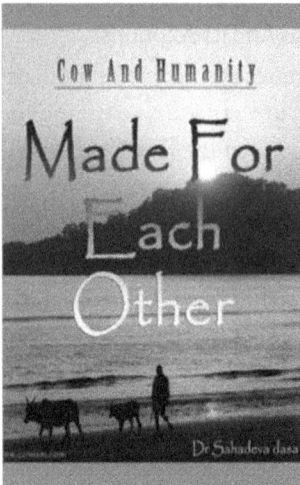

This book discusses the vital role of cows in maintaining peace and prosperity in human society. It also addresses the modern ecological concerns.

It emphasizes the point that 'eCOWlogy' is the original God made ecology. Living with cow is living on nature's income instead of squandering her capital. In the universal scheme of creation, fate of humans has been attached to that of cows, to an absolute and overwhelming degree. Pages-144, www.cowism.com

ISBN 978-81-909760-3-9

Modern Foods - Stealing Years From Your Life

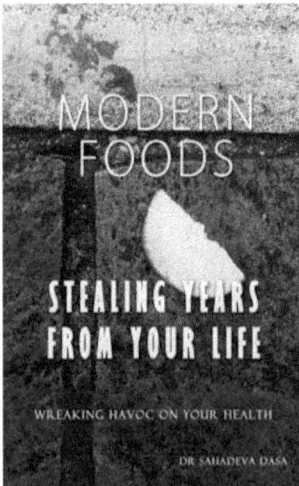

Food is our common ground, a universal experience. But there is trouble with our food. Traditional societies had good food but we have good table manners. A disease tsunami is sweeping the world. Humanity is dying out. This is the result of our deep ignorance about our food. If you don't have good health, the other things like food, housing, transportation, education and recreation don't mean much. This books lists out major killer foods of our industrial civilization and how to escape them. It's a bible on the science of eating. Pages 330, www.farcefood.com, healthrealwealth.com

Cow Are Cool - Love 'Em

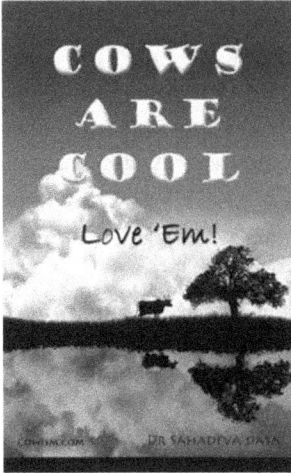

This book deals with the internal lives of the cows and contains true stories from around the world. Cow is a sober animal and does not wag its tail often as a dog. This does not mean dog is good and cow is food. All animals including the dog should be shown love and care. But cow especially has a serious significance for human existence in this world. Talk about cows' feelings is often brushed off as fluffy and sentimental but this book proves it otherwise.

Pages 136, www.cowism.com

ISBN 978-81-909760-4-6

Capitalism Communism & Cowism - A New Economics For The 21st Century

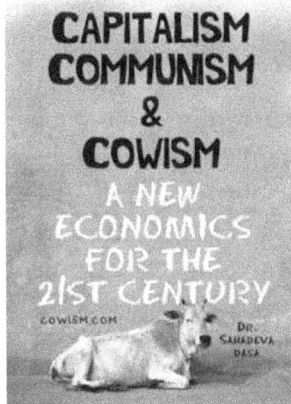

If humanity and the planet have to survive, we have to replace our present day economic model. It's a fossil fuel based, car-centred, energy inefficient model and promotes over exploitation of natural resources, encourages a throwaway society, creates social injustice and is not viable any longer.

This book presents an alternative economic system for the 21st Century. This economic works for the people and the planet.

Pages 172, www.cowism.com,

ISBN 978-81-909760-6-0

Noble Cow - Munching Grass, Looking Curious And Just Hanging Around

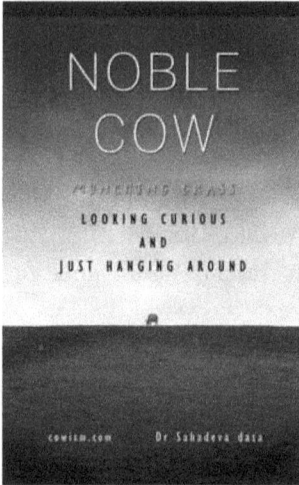

In Taiwan, a cow separated from owner, goes on hunger strike. In rural Cambodia, a motherless child finds mother in a cow as he suckles her. Down in Australia a flood heroine, after rescuing her owner, is leading a pampered existence. In Brazil's Pantanal swamps, a cow was seen wandering among the crocodiles while in India, the land of holy cows, a bull hero is booked out for two years. Up in Alps, the Swiss are combating stress by renting out the mountain cows while in Germany, the nation's focus has been on Yvonne, the runaway cow. There are numerous such stories here. Cows rule and cow rock! Pages 144, Cowism.com, ISBN 978-81-909760-8-4

We Feel Just Like You Do

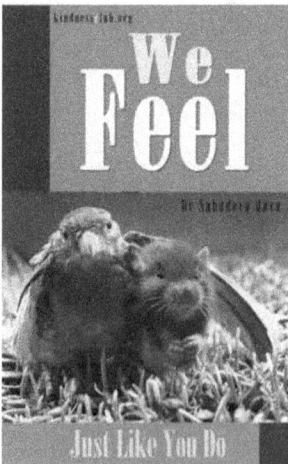

Its enormously puzzling that extreme suffering only gets widely questioned if it is the suffering of members of the human species. It is extraordinary how many people just accept the appalling treatment of such a vast number of animals.
Animals have souls and we have a duty to respect them! Anything less is to deny one's humanity and one's own soul!
Numerous stories outlined in this book prove this point, beyond the shadow of a doubt. Pages 144, KindnessClub.org ISBN 978-81-909760-7-7